SCOTT FORESMAN • ADDISON WESLEY
Mathematics

Math Diagnosis and Intervention System

Booklet H

Fractions in Grades 4–6

Overview of Math Diagnosis and Intervention System

The system can be used in a variety of situations:

- **During school** Use the system for intervention on prerequisite skills at the beginning of the year, the beginning of a chapter, or the beginning of a lesson. Use for intervention during the chapter when more is needed beyond the resources already provided for the lesson.
- **After-school, Saturday-school, summer-school (intersession) programs** Use the system for intervention offered in special programs. The booklets are also available as workbooks.

The system provides resources for:

- **Assessment** For each of Grades K–6, a Diagnostic Test is provided that assesses that grade. Use a test at the start of the year for entry-level assessment or anytime during the year as a summative evaluation.
- **Diagnosis** An item analysis identifies areas where intervention is needed.
- **Intervention** Booklets A–M identify specific topics and assign a number to each topic, for example, A12 or E10. For each topic, there is a page of Intervention Practice and a two-page Intervention Lesson that cover the same content taught in a lesson of the program.
- **Monitoring** The Teaching Guide provides both Individual Record Forms and Class Record Forms to monitor student progress.

Editorial Offices: Glenview, Illinois • Parsippany, New Jersey • New York, New York

Sales Offices: Parsippany, New Jersey • Duluth, Georgia • Glenview, Illinois
Coppell, Texas • Ontario, California • Mesa, Arizona

ISBN: 0-328-07651-1

Copyright © Pearson Education, Inc.
All Rights Reserved. Printed in the United States of America. This publication or parts thereof, may be used with appropriate equipment to reproduce copies for classroom use only.

4 5 6 7 8 9 10 V084 12 11 10 09 08 07 06 05

Table of Contents

		Intervention Lesson Pages	Intervention Practice Pages	\multicolumn{4}{l}{The same content is taught in the Scott Foresman-Addison Wesley Mathematics Program}
				Gr. 3	Gr. 4	Gr. 5	Gr. 6
Booklet H							
Number Theory							
H1	Multiples, Factors, and Divisibility	1	87		7-11		3-1
H2	Factoring Numbers	3	88			3-10	
H3	Prime Factorization	5	89			3-11	3-2
H4	Greatest Common Factor	7	90			7-9	3-3
H5	Least Common Multiple	9	91				3-4
Understanding Fractions							
H6	Equal Parts of a Whole	11	92	9-1			
H7	Naming Fractional Parts	13	93	9-2			
H8	Finding Equivalent Fractions	15	94	9-3	9-6	7-7	
H9	Comparing and Ordering Fractions	17	95	9-4			
H10	Estimating Fractional Amounts	19	96	9-5	9-4		
H11	Fractions on the Number Line	21	97	9-6			
H12	Parts of a Region	23	98		9-1	7-1	3-6
H13	Fractions and Sets	25	99	9-7, 9-8			
H14	Parts of a Set	27	100		9-2	7-1	3-6
H15	Mixed Numbers	29	101	9-10	9-10	7-3	3-8
H16	Fractions on a Number Line	31	102		9-3		
H17	Simplest Form	33	103		9-7	7-10	
H18	Using Number Sense to Compare Fractions	35	104		9-8	7-11	
H19	Comparing and Ordering Fractions	37	105		9-9		
H20	Comparing and Ordering Fractions and Mixed Numbers	39	106		9-11	7-12	
H21	Fractions and Division	41	107			7-2	3-10
H22	Estimating Fractional Amounts	43	108			7-4	3-9
H23	Fractions and Mixed Numbers on the Number Line	45	109			7-5	
H24	Equivalent Fractions	47	110			7-8	3-7
H25	Relating Fractions and Decimals	49	111			7-13	
H26	Fractions, Decimals, and the Number Line	51	112			7-14	3-11

Table of Contents continued

		Intervention Lesson Pages	Intervention Practice Pages	\multicolumn{4}{l}{The same content is taught in the Scott Foresman-Addison Wesley Mathematics Program}
Booklet H				Gr. 3	Gr. 4	Gr. 5	Gr. 6
\multicolumn{8}{l}{**Adding and Subtracting Fractions and Mixed Numbers**}
H27	Adding and Subtracting Fractions	53	113	9-9			
H28	Estimating Fraction Sums and Differences	55	114		10-1		
H29	Adding and Subtracting Fractions with Like Denominators	57	115		10-2, 10-4	8-1	4-1
H30	Least Common Denominator	59	116			8-3	
H31	Adding and Subtracting Fractions with Unlike Denominators	61	117		10-3, 10-5	8-2, 8-4	4-2
H32	Investigating Adding and Subtracting Mixed Numbers	63	118			8-5	
H33	Estimating Sums and Differences of Mixed Numbers	65	119			8-6	4-4
H34	Adding Mixed Numbers	67	120			8-7	4-5
H35	Subtracting Mixed Numbers	69	121			8-8	4-6
H36	Choose a Computation Method	71	122				4-7
\multicolumn{8}{l}{**Multiplying and Dividing Fractions and Mixed Numbers**}
H37	Multiplying Fractions by Whole Numbers	73	123			8-10	5-1
H38	Estimating Products	75	124			8-11	5-3
H39	Multiplying by a Fraction	77	125			8-12	5-2
H40	Multiplying Fractions and Mixed Numbers	79	126			8-13	5-4
H41	Understanding Division with Fractions	81	127			8-14	
H42	Dividing Fractions	83	128				5-6
H43	Multiplying and Dividing Mixed Numbers	85	129				5-7

Intervention Lesson **H1**

Multiples, Factors, and Divisibility

Example

Use the divisibility rules to decide if 144 is divisible by the following numbers.

Number	Divisibility Rule	Is 144 divisible?	Explanation
2	The last digit is even. 0, 2, 4, 6, or 8	Yes	144 is even
3	Sum of the digits is divisible by 3.	Yes	$1 + 4 + 4 = 9$ $9 \div 3 = 3$
4	The last two digits of the number are divisible by 4.	Yes	The last two digits of 144 are 44 and $44 \div 4 = 11$
5	The ones digit is a 0 or 5.	No	The last digit is 4, not 0 or 5.
6	The number is divisible by 2 and 3.	Yes	144 is divisible by 2 and 3
9	Sum of the digits is divisible by 9.	Yes	$1 + 4 + 4 = 9$ $9 \div 9 = 1$
10	The ones digit is 0.	No	Last digit is 4, not 0.

A **multiple** of a number is the product of the number and a whole number greater than 0. 20 is a multiple of 4; $4 \times 5 = 20$

When a number is divided by any of its **factors,** or divisors, the remainder is 0. 4 is a factor of 20.

Test each number to see if it is divisible by 2, 3, 4, 5, 6, 9, or 10.

1. 56 **2.** 78 **3.** 182 **4.** 380

_____ _____ _____ _____

5. 105 **6.** 126 **7.** 430 **8.** 635

_____ _____ _____ _____

1

Name _____

Intervention Lesson **H1**

Math Diagnosis and Intervention System

Multiples, Factors, and Divisibility (continued)

Test each number to see if it is divisible by 2, 3, 4, 5, 6, 9, or 10.

9. 45   **10.** 88   **11.** 96   **12.** 102

_____ _____ _____ _____

13. 214   **14.** 313   **15.** 425   **16.** 670

_____ _____ _____ _____

17. 845   **18.** 400   **19.** 900   **20.** 1,002

_____ _____ _____ _____

21. 2,580   **22.** 3,470   **23.** 4,311   **24.** 8,356

_____ _____ _____ _____

Tell whether the first number is a multiple of the second.

25. 105; 5   **26.** 212; 6   **27.** 3,006; 9   **28.** 1,010; 10

_____ _____ _____ _____

29. Camp Many Lakes has 198 campers registered this year. They are planning many activities and games which must be completed in groups. Into what different sizes of groups could Camp Many Lakes divide the campers into?   _____

30. Writing in Math Are all numbers divisible by 5 also divisible by 10? How do you know? Are all numbers that are divisible by 10, also divisible by 5? How do you know?

_____

_____

Test Prep Circle the correct letter for the answer.

31. Which number is divisible by 3, 5 and 10?

   A 10   **B** 25   **C** 30   **D** 42

32. Which number is a multiple of 9?

   A 468   **B** 523   **C** 601   **D** 1,209

Name _____

Math Diagnosis and Intervention System

Intervention Lesson **H2**

Factoring Numbers

Example 1

Find all the factors of 12.
Factors of 12: 1, 2, 3, 4, 6, 12

Example 2

Is 3 a factor of 72?

Divide 72 by 3.
If the remainder is 0, then 3 is a factor.

3 is a factor of 72.

$$\begin{array}{r} 24 \\ 3\overline{)72} \\ -6 \\ \hline 12 \\ -12 \\ \hline 0 \end{array}$$

Find all the factors of each number. Tell whether each is prime or composite.

1. 7

2. 8

3. 21

4. 48

5. 51

6. 9

7. 17

8. 26

9. 40

3

Math Diagnosis and Intervention System

Intervention Lesson **H2**

Name _____

Factoring Numbers (continued)

Find all the factors of each number. Tell whether each is prime or composite.

10. 55   **11.** 70   **12.** 83

_____ _____ _____

_____ _____ _____

13. Is 4 a factor of 48? ____   **14.** Is 18 divisible by 8? ____

15. Is 7 a factor of 91? ____   **16.** Is 74 divisible by 6? ____

Write each number as a product of two or more factors in as many ways as possible.

17. 18   **18.** 25   **19.** 35

_____ _____ _____

_____ _____ _____

20. Mr. Lee has 18 desks in his room. He would like them arranged in a rectangular array. Draw all the different possible arrays and write a multiplication sentence for each.

Test Prep Circle the correct letter for the answer.

21. Find the number that is not a factor of 24.

    A 3   **B** 4   **C** 5   **D** 6

22. Which number is divisible by 9?

    A 28   **B** 49   **C** 56   **D** 63

Intervention Lesson **H3**

Prime Factorization

Example

Use a factor tree to find the prime factorization of 240. Then write the product using exponents.

Write 240 as a product of two factors. This can be done in more than one way. Write each factor that is not prime as a product.

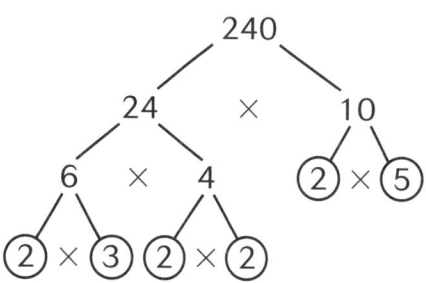

When all the branches end in prime numbers, you can write the prime factorization. The primes are usually written from least to greatest. Whenever factors appear more than once, exponents can be used.

$240 = 2^4 \times 3 \times 5$

Complete each factor tree. Write the prime factorization with exponents, if you can.

1.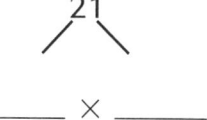

____ × ____

____

2.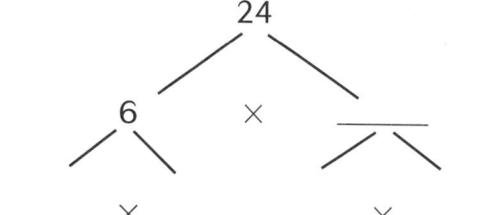

____ × ____ ____ × ____

____

3.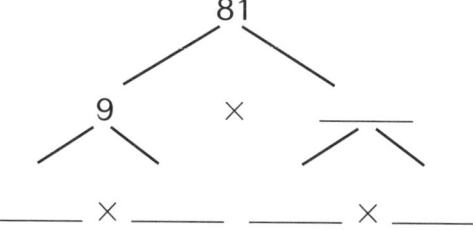

____ × ____ ____ × ____

____

4.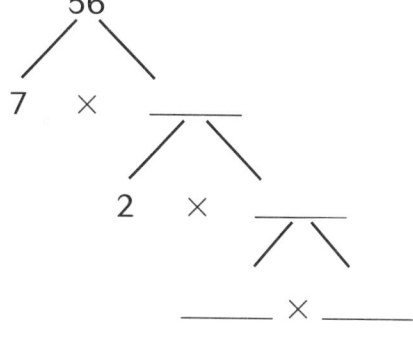

____ × ____

5

Name _____   Intervention Lesson **H3**

Prime Factorization (continued)

Draw two different factor trees for each number.

5.   45   **6.**   36   **7.**   42

If the number is prime, write <u>prime</u>. If the number is composite, write the prime factorization of the number.

8. 11   **9.** 18   **10.** 41   **11.** 40

_____   _____   _____   _____

12. 16   **13.** 17   **14.** 80   **15.** 95

_____   _____   _____   _____

16. 35   **17.** 72   **18.** 48   **19.** 55

_____   _____   _____   _____

20. Math Reasoning What number has a prime factorization of $2^3 \times 7$?

_____

21. Holly says the prime factorization for 44 is 4×11. Is she right? Why or why not?

_____

Test Prep Circle the correct letter for the answer.

22. Find the prime factorization for 12.

   A 4×3 **B** 2×3 **C** $2^2 \times 3$ **D** 2×3^2

23. Find the prime number:

   A 55   **B** 15   **C** 41   **D** 39

Name _____

Intervention Lesson **H4**

Greatest Common Factor

Example

List the common factors of 20 and 32. Then find the greatest common factor of the pair of numbers.

Factors of 20: 1, 2, 4, 5, 10, 20
Factors of 32: 1, 2, 4, 8, 16, 32

Common factors are 1, 2, and 4.
The greatest common factor is 4.

Find the greatest common factor (GCF).

1. 12, 14
GCF: _____

2. 15, 20
GCF: _____

3. 32, 24
GCF: _____

4. 15, 27
GCF: _____

5. 7, 21
GCF: _____

6. 42, 35
GCF: _____

7. 8, 32
GCF: _____

8. 36, 25
GCF: _____

9. 30, 40
GCF: _____

10. 17, 64
GCF: _____

11. 12, 36
GCF: _____

12. 26, 38
GCF: _____

13. 15, 24
GCF: _____

14. 8, 23
GCF: _____

15. 60, 70
GCF: _____

16. 35, 70
GCF: _____

Name _____   Intervention Lesson **H4**

Greatest Common Factor (continued)

Find the greatest common factor (GCF).

17. 8, 12　　　**18.** 16, 20　　　**19.** 15, 25　　　**20.** 18, 45

_____　　　_____　　　_____　　　_____

21. 35, 81　　　**22.** 21, 24　　　**23.** 34, 40　　　**24.** 7, 31

_____　　　_____　　　_____　　　_____

25. 6, 42　　　**26.** 8, 32, 40　　　**27.** 35, 42, 70　　　**28.** 10, 35, 75

_____　　　_____　　　_____　　　_____

29. Math Reasoning Find two numbers whose greatest common factor is 12.

_____

30. Hope says the greatest common factor for 12 and 36 is 6. Is she right? Why or why not?

_____

31. A teacher has 35 desks in her room and 45 books. What is the greatest number of rows she can have if she wishes to have the same number of desks and books in each row?

_____

Test Prep Circle the correct letter for the answer.

32. Find the greatest common factor for 14 and 28.

　　A 2　　　**B** 7　　　**C** 14　　　**D** 28

Least Common Multiple

Intervention Lesson H5

Example

List the first several multiples of 15 and 6. Then find common multiples and the least common multiple (LCM).

Multiples of 15: 15, 30, 45, 60, 75, 90

Multiples of 6: 6, 12, 18, 24, 30, 36, 42, 48, 54, 60

Common multiples are 30, 60, ...
The least common multiple is 30.

You can also use prime factorization, particularly with large numbers.

$15 = 3 \times 5$
$6 = 3 \times 2$
$LCM = 3 \times 5 \times 2 = 30$

Find the least common multiple (LCM).

1. 2, 5
   LCM: ____

2. 15, 10
   LCM: ____

3. 3, 4
   LCM: ____

4. 5, 8
   LCM: ____

5. 7, 21
   LCM: ____

6. 15, 25
   LCM: ____

7. 8, 10
   LCM: ____

8. 6, 9
   LCM: ____

9. 30, 4
   LCM: ____

10. 18, 9
    LCM: ____

11. 12, 36
    LCM: ____

12. 22, 4
    LCM: ____

Name _____

Intervention Lesson **H5**

Least Common Multiple (continued)

Find the least common multiple (LCM).

13. 6, 12

14. 8, 20

15. 3, 14

16. 8, 6

17. 10, 14

18. 7, 12

19. 3, 42

20. 15, 9

21. 6, 25

22. 8, 12, 15

23. 3, 4, 5

24. 10, 12, 15

25. Math Reasoning Find two numbers whose least common multiple is 12.

26. A student group is having a large cookout. They wish to buy the same number of hamburgers and hamburger buns. Hamburgers come in packages of 12 and buns come in packages of 8. What is the least amount of each they can buy in order to have the same amount?

Test Prep Circle the correct letter for the answer.

27. Find the least common multiple for 24 and 27.

A 3   **B** 24   **C** 72   **D** 216

10

Name _____

Intervention Lesson **H6**

Equal Parts of a Whole

Example

A whole can be divided into equal parts in different ways.

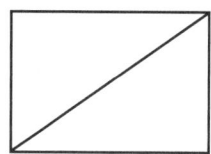 __2__ equal parts
The equal parts are
named __halves__.

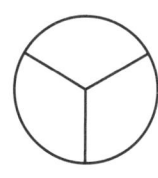 __3__ equal parts
The equal parts are
named __thirds__.

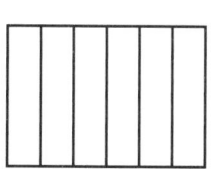 __6__ equal parts
The equal parts are
named __sixths__.

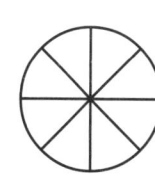 __8__ equal parts
The equal parts are
named __eighths__.

Tell how many parts. Then tell if each shows equal parts or unequal parts.

1. 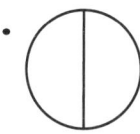 __2__ parts

   __equal parts__

2. 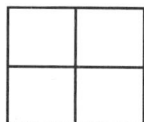 _____ parts

3.  _____ parts

4. 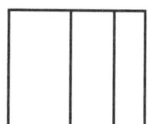 _____ parts

5.  _____ parts

6.  _____ parts

11

Name _____

Intervention Lesson **H6**

Math Diagnosis and Intervention System

Equal Parts of a Whole (continued)

Tell if each shows equal parts or unequal parts.

7. 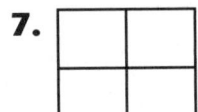 _____

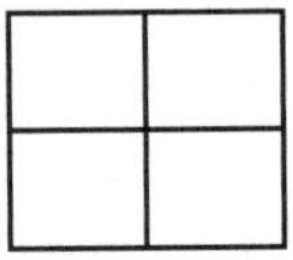

8.  _____

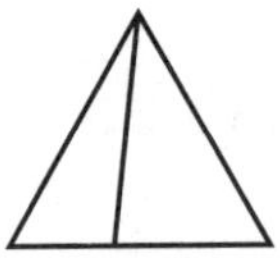

9.  _____

10. 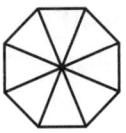 _____

11. 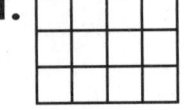 _____

12. 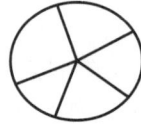 _____

13.  _____

14. 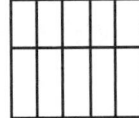 _____

Name the equal parts of the whole.

15. 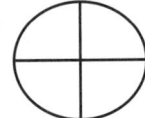 _____

16. 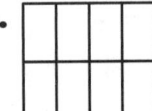 _____

17.  _____

18.  _____

19. **Reasoning** If 5 children want to share a large pizza and each gets 2 pieces, will they need to cut the pizza into fifths, eighths, or tenths? _____

Test Prep Circle the correct letter for the answer.

20.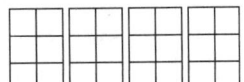

Which names the equal parts of the rectangle?

    A sixths   **B** thirds   **C** fifths   **D** fourths

Name _____

Math Diagnosis and Intervention System

Intervention Lesson **H7**

Naming Fractional Parts

Example 1

Name the fraction of the rectangle that is shaded.

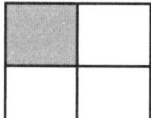 one part shaded   1 ← **numerator** tells how many equal parts are shaded

4 equal parts in all   4 ← **denominator** tells how many equal parts in all

$\frac{1}{4}$ of the rectangle is shaded.   **One fourth** of the rectangle is shaded.

Example 2

Name the fraction of the circle that is shaded.

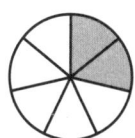 $\frac{2}{7}$ ← **numerator** (number of equal parts shaded)
← **denominator** (number of equal parts in all)

$\frac{2}{7}$ of the circle is shaded.   **Two sevenths** of the circle is shaded.

---

1. If 2 parts of the rectangle were shaded in Example 1, what fraction of the rectangle would be shaded?

_____

2. If only one equal part of the circle was shaded in Example 2, what fraction of the circle would be shaded?

_____

13

Name _____

Intervention Lesson **H7**

Naming Fractional Parts (continued)

Shade the figure to show the fraction.

3. $\frac{3}{4}$    4. $\frac{3}{6}$ 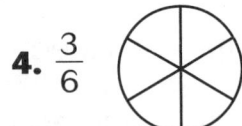   5. $\frac{5}{8}$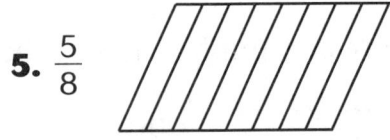

Write the fraction of each figure that is shaded.

6. 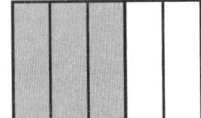   7. 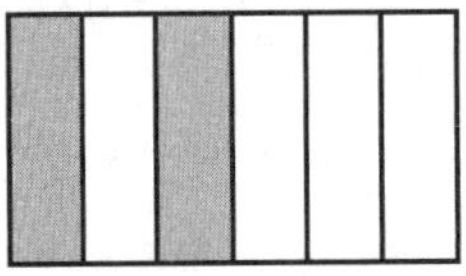 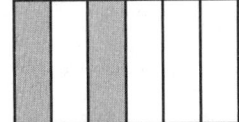   8.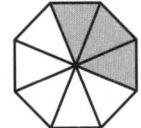

_____   _____   _____

Draw a picture to show each fraction.

9. three fourths   10. $\frac{4}{6}$ 11. $\frac{2}{2}$

  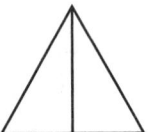

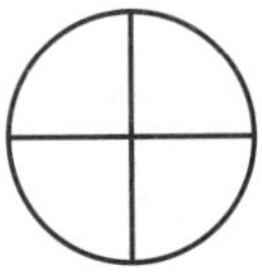

12. **Reasoning** Lyle cut a pizza into 8 pieces. He ate 2 pieces, and his brother ate 3 pieces. Write the fraction that tells what part of the whole pizza was eaten. _____

Test Prep Circle the correct letter for each answer.

13. What fraction of the figure is shaded?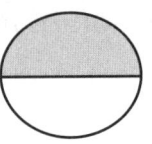

   A $\frac{1}{3}$ **B** $\frac{1}{2}$ **C** $\frac{2}{2}$ **D** $\frac{1}{4}$

14. A quilt is made from 12 equal-sized squares of cloth. Four of the squares are yellow. What fraction of the quilt is yellow?

   A $\frac{4}{12}$ **B** $\frac{4}{10}$ **C** $\frac{1}{2}$ **D** $\frac{2}{3}$

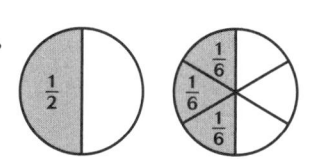

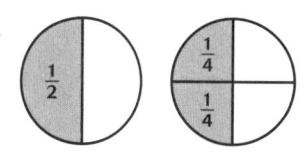

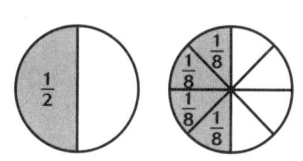

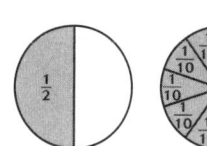

Finding Equivalent Fractions

Example

Find equivalent fractions. $\dfrac{3}{4} = \dfrac{6}{8}$

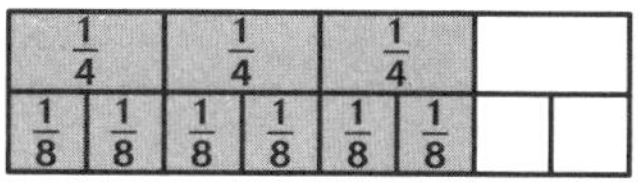

Find equivalent fractions.

1. $\dfrac{}{4} = \dfrac{}{8}$

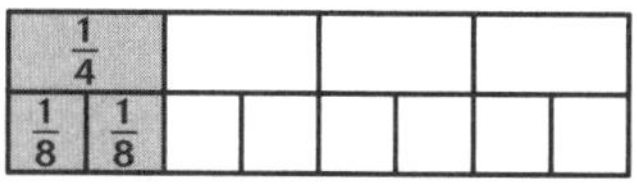

2. $\dfrac{}{2} = \dfrac{}{6}$

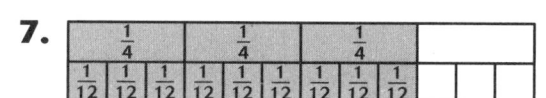

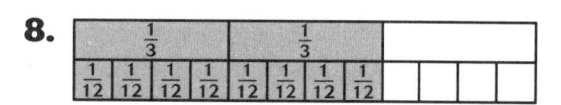

3. $\dfrac{}{2} = \dfrac{}{4}$

4. $\dfrac{}{3} = \dfrac{}{6}$

5. $\dfrac{}{2} = \dfrac{}{8}$

6. $\dfrac{}{2} = \dfrac{}{10}$

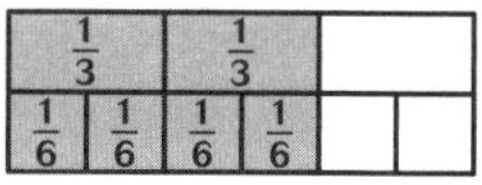

7. $\dfrac{}{4} = \dfrac{}{12}$

8. $\dfrac{}{3} = \dfrac{}{12}$

9. $\dfrac{}{6} = \dfrac{}{12}$

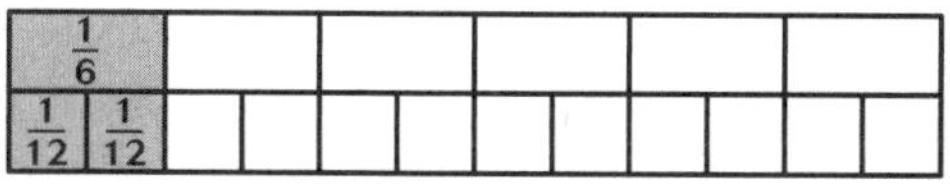

Math Diagnosis and Intervention System

Intervention Lesson **H8**

Name _____

Finding Equivalent Fractions (continued)

10.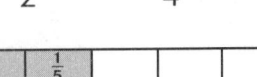

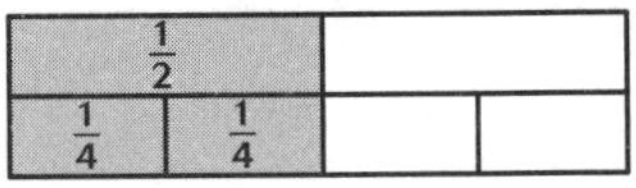

$$\frac{\ }{2} = \frac{\ }{4}$$

11.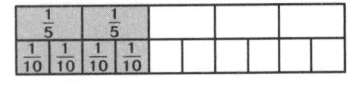

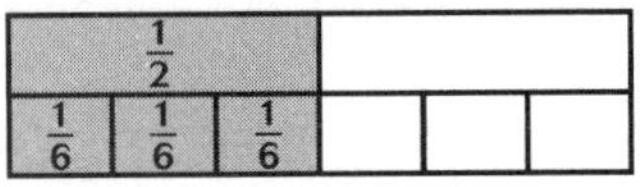

$$\frac{\ }{2} = \frac{\ }{6}$$

12.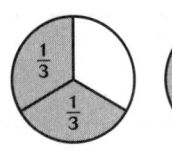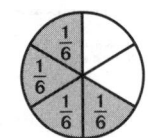

$$\frac{\ }{3} = \frac{\ }{6}$$

13.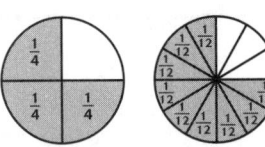

$$\frac{\ }{5} = \frac{\ }{10}$$

14.

$$\frac{\ }{4} = \frac{\ }{12}$$

15.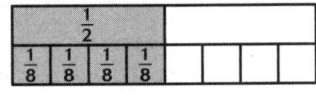

$$\frac{\ }{2} = \frac{\ }{8}$$

16. **Reasoning** Use fraction strips to show that $\frac{1}{3}$ is the same as $\frac{2}{6}$.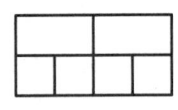

17. On Tuesday, $\frac{2}{3}$ of the class time was spent on math projects. How many sixths of the class time was spent on math projects? _____

18. Video A is $\frac{3}{4}$ of an hour in length. Video B is $\frac{6}{8}$ of an hour in length. Which video is longer? _____

Test Prep Circle the correct letter for the answer.

19. Which fraction is equivalent to $\frac{1}{4}$?

    A $\frac{1}{8}$ B $\frac{2}{4}$ C $\frac{2}{8}$ D $\frac{3}{8}$

Name _____

Intervention Lesson **H9**

Math Diagnosis and Intervention System

Comparing and Ordering Fractions

Example

You can use fraction strips or fraction circles to compare fractions with different denominators.

Compare: $\frac{4}{5}$ ● $\frac{2}{3}$

| $\frac{1}{5}$ | $\frac{1}{5}$ | $\frac{1}{5}$ | $\frac{1}{5}$ | |
| $\frac{1}{3}$ | $\frac{1}{3}$ | | | |

So, $\frac{4}{5} > \frac{2}{3}$.

Compare. Write >, <, or = for each ●.

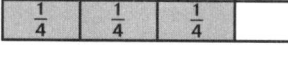

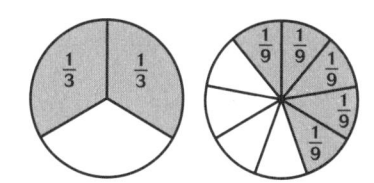

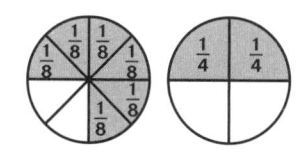

1. $\frac{1}{4}$ ● $\frac{3}{4}$

2. $\frac{5}{10}$ ● $\frac{3}{10}$

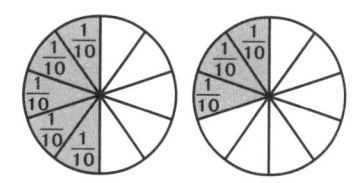

3. $\frac{2}{3}$ ● $\frac{5}{9}$

4. $\frac{1}{5}$ ● $\frac{5}{10}$

5. $\frac{6}{8}$ ● $\frac{2}{4}$

6. $\frac{3}{4}$ ● $\frac{2}{8}$

17

Name _____

Math Diagnosis and Intervention System

Intervention Lesson **H9**

Comparing and Ordering Fractions (continued)

Compare. Write >, <, or = for each ●.

7. $\frac{3}{5}$ ● $\frac{1}{4}$

8. $\frac{2}{3}$ ● $\frac{4}{6}$

9. $\frac{2}{8}$ ● $\frac{1}{4}$

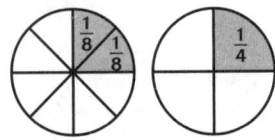

10. $\frac{7}{8}$ ● $\frac{3}{4}$

11. $\frac{1}{3}$ ● $\frac{3}{5}$

12. $\frac{1}{2}$ ● $\frac{2}{6}$

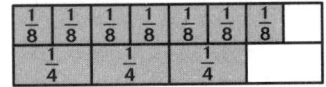 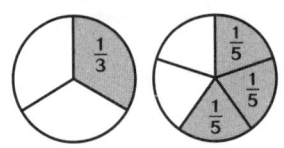 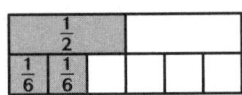

Write each set of fractions in order from least to greatest.

13. $\frac{1}{4}, \frac{6}{7}, \frac{3}{5}$

14. $\frac{5}{8}, \frac{1}{2}, \frac{3}{4}$

15. $\frac{1}{2}, \frac{5}{6}, \frac{2}{3}$

16. $\frac{3}{9}, \frac{1}{4}, \frac{5}{6}$

_____ _____ _____ _____

17. **Reasoning** Give 3 fractions with different denominators that are less than $\frac{4}{6}$. _____

18. Two students are writing stories. Eric's story is $\frac{2}{3}$ of a page. Jason's story is $\frac{4}{6}$ of a page. Whose story is longer?

_____

Test Prep Circle the correct letter for the answer.

19. Which fraction is greater than $\frac{2}{3}$?

    A $\frac{1}{3}$ **B** $\frac{4}{6}$ **C** $\frac{3}{6}$ **D** $\frac{5}{6}$

Name _____

Math Diagnosis and Intervention System

Intervention Lesson **H10**

Estimating Fractional Amounts

Example

Estimate fractional amounts.
Think of fractions you know. Then compare.

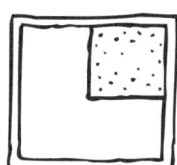

Think		Compare
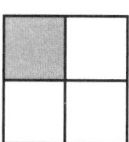	$\frac{1}{4}$	about $\frac{1}{4}$ left
 	$\frac{2}{3}$	about $\frac{2}{3}$ full
 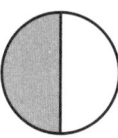	$\frac{1}{2}$	about $\frac{1}{2}$ left

1. Estimate the fraction of the pie that is left.

_____

2. About what fraction of the pie was eaten? _____

Estimate the amount that is left.

3.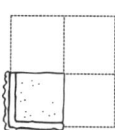

_____   _____   _____   _____

19

Name _____

Math Diagnosis and Intervention System

Intervention Lesson **H10**

Estimating Fractional Amounts (continued)

Estimate how much orange juice is in each glass. Write the amount.

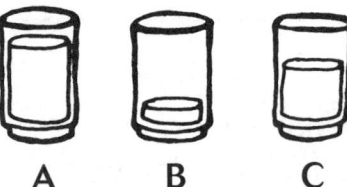

A   B   C

4. Glass B _____

5. Glass A _____

6. Circle the estimate of how much time has passed since 8:00.

About $\frac{1}{2}$ hour   About $\frac{1}{4}$ hour

About $\frac{1}{5}$ hour   About 1 hour

Estimate the amount that is shaded.

7. 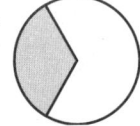 _____

8. 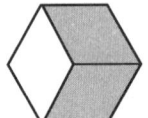 _____

9. Reasoning Marcia and Isabel bought a pizza. Marcia ate $\frac{1}{2}$ of the pizza, and Isabel ate $\frac{1}{4}$ of it. What fraction of the pizza is left? _____

Test Prep Circle the correct letter for the answer.

10. About how much of the lemonade is left if the glass was full?

A $\frac{1}{3}$ B $\frac{1}{2}$ C $\frac{2}{3}$ D $\frac{1}{4}$

Intervention Lesson **H11**

Fractions on the Number Line

Example

Use fractions to name points on a number line.
Write the missing fractions for the number line.

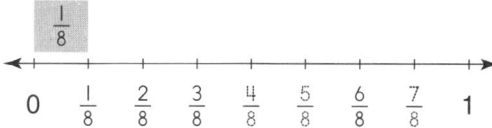

Think: The distance between 0 and 1 is divided into eighths.

Count: $\frac{1}{8}, \frac{2}{8}, \frac{3}{8}, \frac{4}{8}, \frac{5}{8}, \frac{6}{8}, \frac{7}{8}, \frac{8}{8}$, or 1.

---

1. What fraction is the distance between 0 and 1 divided? _____
Write the missing fractions for the number line.

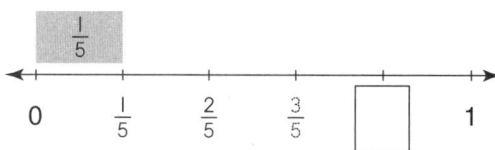

2. What fraction is the distance between 0 and 1 divided? _____
Write the missing fractions for the number line.

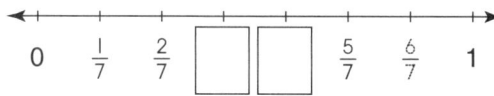

21

Name _____

Intervention Lesson **H11**

Fractions on the Number Line (continued)

Write the missing fractions for each number line.

3.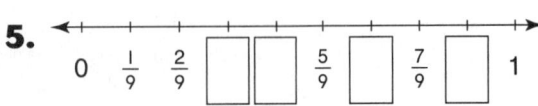

4.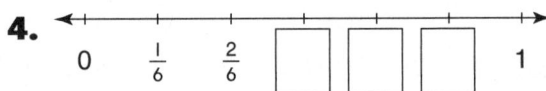

5.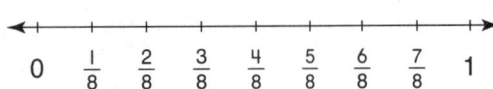

Use the number line to compare fractions.

0 $\frac{1}{8}$ $\frac{2}{8}$ $\frac{3}{8}$ $\frac{4}{8}$ $\frac{5}{8}$ $\frac{6}{8}$ $\frac{7}{8}$ 1

6. Which is greater, $\frac{3}{8}$ or $\frac{5}{8}$? _____

7. Which is less, $\frac{2}{8}$ or $\frac{4}{8}$? _____

8. **Reasoning** Glen ran a 1-mile race. Ned and Lois ran as far as they could in the race.

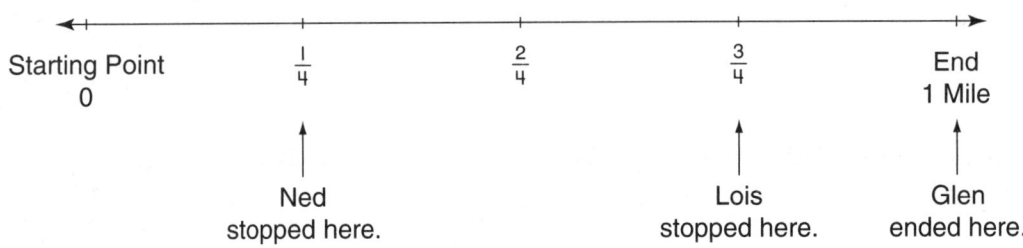

9. Write a fraction that shows how far Ned and Lois ran.

   Ned _____   Lois _____

Test Prep Circle the correct letter for each answer.

10. In the race above, how much farther did Glen run than Lois?

    A $\frac{1}{2}$ mile **B** $\frac{1}{4}$ mile **C** $\frac{2}{4}$ mile **D** 1 mile

11. What number shows how far Glen ran?

    A $\frac{1}{2}$ mile **B** $\frac{1}{4}$ mile **C** $\frac{2}{4}$ mile **D** 1 mile

Name _____

Intervention Lesson **H12**

Parts of a Region

Example

Write the fraction for the shaded part of the region.

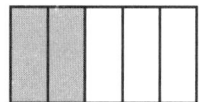

$\dfrac{2}{5} = \dfrac{\text{number of equal parts shaded}}{\text{total number of equal parts}}$

So, $\dfrac{2}{5}$ of the region is shaded.

Write the fraction for the shaded parts of each region.

1.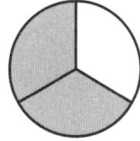

   _____

2.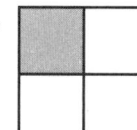

   _____

3.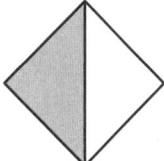

   _____

4.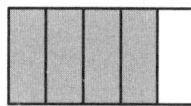

   _____

5.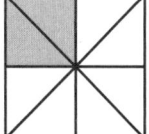

   _____

6.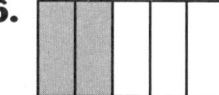

   _____

Name _____

Math Diagnosis and Intervention System
Intervention Lesson **H12**

Parts of a Region (continued)

Write the fraction for the shaded parts of each region.

7.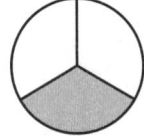

8.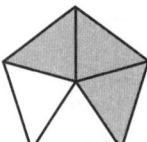

9.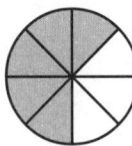

_____   _____   _____

Draw a picture to show each fraction.

10. $\frac{1}{5}$ 11. $\frac{2}{3}$ 12. $\frac{7}{8}$ 13. $\frac{4}{7}$

14. $\frac{5}{8}$ 15. $\frac{6}{6}$ 16. $\frac{2}{8}$ 17. $\frac{4}{5}$

18. **Math Reasoning** Draw a picture to show $\frac{1}{3}$. Then divide each of the parts in half. What fraction of the parts does the $\frac{1}{3}$ represent now? _____

19. Ben divided a pie into 8 equal pieces and ate 3 of them. How much of the pie remains? _____

Test Prep Circle the correct letter for the answer.

20. There are 4 yards the same size on Ramsey Street. Three of the yards were mowed today. How much of Ramsey Street was left unmowed?

  A $\frac{3}{4}$ **B** $\frac{1}{4}$ **C** $\frac{4}{3}$ **D** $\frac{1}{3}$

24

Intervention Lesson **H13**

Fractions and Sets

Example 1

What fraction of the set, or group, of counters is circled?

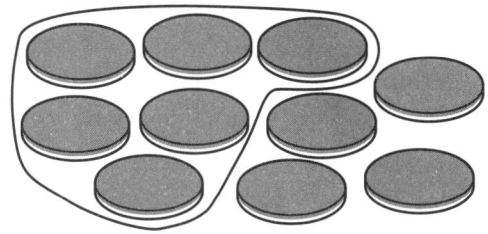

Number of circled counters → **6**

Total number of counters → **10**

$\frac{6}{10}$ of the counters are circled.

Example 2

Find $\frac{1}{3}$ of 12.

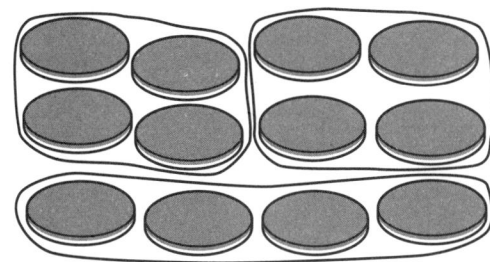

Think about division to find a fraction of a number.

Think: Divide 12 into 3 equal groups.

$12 \div 3 = 4$

Write: $\frac{1}{3}$ of 12 = 4

Write a fraction to tell what part of the set, or group, is circled.

1. 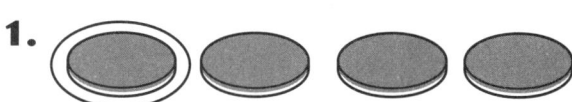 _____

2.  _____

3. Find $\frac{1}{4}$ of 16.

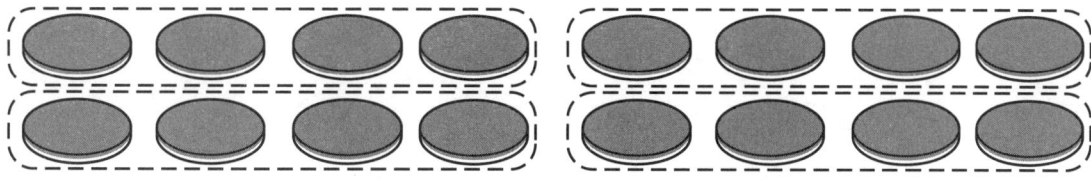

$\frac{1}{4}$ of 16 = _____

25

Name _____

Intervention Lesson **H13**

Fractions and Sets (continued)

4. Find $\frac{1}{2}$ of 6.

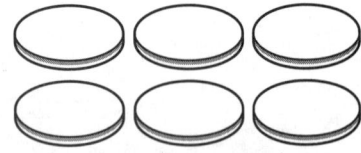

6 ÷ 2 = _____

$\frac{1}{2}$ of 6 = _____

5. Find $\frac{1}{4}$ of 12.

12 ÷ 4 = _____

$\frac{1}{4}$ of 12 = _____

6. Find $\frac{1}{3}$ of 27.

_____

7. Find $\frac{1}{8}$ of 24.

_____

8. Shade the counters to show $\frac{2}{5}$ of a group.

9. Number Sense Suppose you slept for $\frac{1}{3}$ of a 24-hour day. How many hours did you sleep? _____

Test Prep Circle the correct letter for the answer.

10. What fraction of the counters are shaded?

A $\frac{4}{6}$ B $\frac{2}{6}$ C $\frac{1}{8}$ D $\frac{2}{8}$

11. Find $\frac{1}{4}$ of 36.

A 9   B 8   C 4   D 6

Name _____

Intervention Lesson **H14**

Parts of a Set

Example

Write the fraction for the shaded parts of the set.

$\dfrac{2}{7} = \dfrac{\text{number of shaded shapes}}{\text{total number of shapes}}$

So, $\dfrac{2}{7}$ of the region is shaded.

Write the fraction for the shaded parts of each set.

1. ▽ △ ▽

   _____

2. ☾ ☾

   _____

3. 🌸 🌸 🌸 ❀

   _____

4. 🍒 🍒 🍒 🍒 🍒

   _____

5. ● ○ ○ ○ ○ ○

   _____

6. ● ○ ○

   _____

27

Name _____

Intervention Lesson **H14**

Parts of a Set (continued)

Write the fraction for the shaded parts of each set.

7. ★ ★ ☆ ☆ ☆   _____

8. ☾☾☾☾☾☾   _____

Draw a set of shapes and shade them to show each fraction.

9. $\frac{6}{8}$

10. $\frac{2}{7}$

11. $\frac{5}{9}$

12. $\frac{6}{10}$

13. $\frac{5}{8}$

14. $\frac{4}{9}$

Test Prep Circle the correct letter for the answer.

15. Find $\frac{1}{4}$ of 12.

    A 3   **B** 4   **C** 9   **D** 8

Intervention Lesson **H15**

Mixed Numbers

Example 1

Write $\frac{14}{3}$ as a mixed number.

Divide the numerator by the denominator.

$$\begin{array}{r} 4 \\ 3\overline{)14} \\ -12 \\ \hline 2 \end{array}$$

Write the quotient as the whole number.
Write the remainder as the numerator of the fraction. $4\frac{2}{3}$
Use the same denominator.

Example 2

Write $2\frac{3}{4}$ as an improper fraction.

Multiply the denominator by the whole number ⟶ 2×4

and add the numerator. ⟶ $+ 3 = 11$

Write the result over the denominator. $\frac{11}{4}$

Change each improper fraction to a mixed number or a whole number and change each mixed number to an improper fraction.

1. $1\frac{2}{5}$ 　　 2. $\frac{5}{3}$ 　　 3. $\frac{7}{6}$ 　　 4. $2\frac{1}{7}$

_____　　_____　　_____　　_____

5. $\frac{9}{3}$ 　　 6. $4\frac{4}{7}$ 　　 7. $\frac{14}{5}$ 　　 8. $5\frac{2}{9}$

_____　　_____　　_____　　_____

29

Math Diagnosis and Intervention System

Intervention Lesson **H15**

Name _____

Mixed Numbers (continued)

Change each improper fraction to a mixed number or a whole number, and change each mixed number to an improper fraction.

9. $3\frac{2}{7}$ 10. $\frac{7}{3}$ 11. $\frac{7}{2}$ 12. $1\frac{1}{10}$

_____   _____   _____   _____

13. $\frac{9}{4}$ 14. $2\frac{2}{7}$ 15. $\frac{14}{2}$ 16. $6\frac{4}{9}$

_____   _____   _____   _____

Write an improper fraction and a mixed number or whole number for each picture.

17. 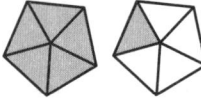   18. 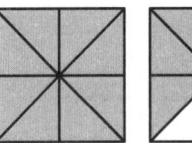   19.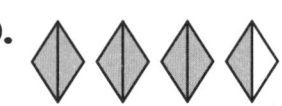

___ ___   ___ ___   ___ ___

20. **Reasoning** If an improper fraction has a numerator and denominator that are equal, then what will the equivalent whole number always be?   _____

21. There are 12 eggs in a carton. Mrs. Hudson has 15 eggs. Use a mixed number to describe how many cartons of eggs Mrs. Hudson has.   _____

Test Prep Circle the correct letter for the answer.

22. Change $\frac{15}{4}$ to a mixed number or whole number.

   A $2\frac{7}{4}$ **B** $3\frac{4}{3}$ **C** 4   **D** $3\frac{3}{4}$

30

Name _____

Intervention Lesson **H16**

Fractions on a Number Line

Example

What fraction should be written at Point A?

There are 6 equal parts between 0 and 1. Point A shows 2 of the 6 equal parts. So, $\frac{2}{6}$ should be written at Point A. The fraction $\frac{2}{6}$ may also be shown as a shaded part of a length.

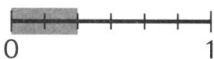

Write a fraction for the part of each length that is shaded.

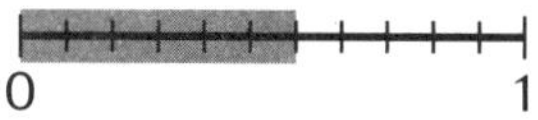

_____   _____   _____

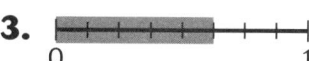

_____   _____   _____

What fraction should be written at each point?

7. Point R _____   **8.** Point S _____   **9.** Point T _____

31

Name _____

Intervention Lesson **H16**

Math Diagnosis and Intervention System

Fractions on a Number Line (continued)

What fraction should be written at each point?

10. Point X _____   **11.** Point y _____   **12.** Point Z _____

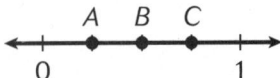

13. Point A _____   **14.** Point B _____   **15.** Point C _____

16. Draw 0 and 1 on a number line. Then show $\frac{3}{7}$ and $\frac{6}{7}$.

17. Number Sense What number is halfway between $\frac{2}{4}$ and $\frac{3}{4}$ on a number line? _____

18. Write the missing measures on the ruler shown.

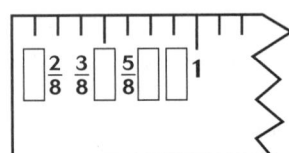

Test Prep Circle the correct letter for the answer.

19. Give the missing fraction:

A $\frac{2}{4}$ B $\frac{1}{4}$ C $\frac{2}{3}$ D $\frac{1}{3}$

32

Name _____

Intervention Lesson **H17**

Simplest Form

Example 1

Anita has 30 flowers. 12 of the flowers are roses. What fraction of the flowers are roses? Write $\frac{12}{30}$ in simplest form.

A fraction is in **simplest form** if its numerator and denominator have no common factors other than 1.

One Way

12 and 30 have the common factor 2.
$\frac{12}{30} \div \frac{2}{2} = \frac{6}{15}$ 6 and 15 have the common factor 3.
$\frac{6}{15} \div \frac{3}{3} = \frac{2}{5}$

Another Way

12 and 30 have the common factor 6.
$\frac{12}{30} \div \frac{6}{6} = \frac{2}{5}$

Example 2

Write $\frac{24}{48}$ in simplest form.

A common factor of 24 and 48 is 6. $\frac{24}{48} \div \frac{6}{6} = \frac{4}{8}$

$\frac{4}{8}$ is not in simplest form. Find another common factor.

4 is a common factor of 4 and 8. $\frac{4}{8} \div \frac{4}{4} = \frac{1}{2}$

Write each fraction in simplest form.

1. $\frac{5}{10}$

2. $\frac{14}{16}$

3. $\frac{27}{45}$

4. $\frac{10}{15}$

33

Name _____

Intervention Lesson **H17**

Simplest Form (continued)

Write each fraction in simplest form. If it is in simplest form, write simplest form.

5. $\frac{5}{20}$ 　　 6. $\frac{14}{18}$ 　　 7. $\frac{5}{11}$ 　　 8. $\frac{1}{15}$

_____ 　　 _____ 　　 _____ 　　 _____

9. $\frac{6}{20}$ 　　 10. $\frac{36}{45}$ 　　 11. $\frac{11}{33}$ 　　 12. $\frac{24}{60}$

_____ 　　 _____ 　　 _____ 　　 _____

13. $\frac{18}{24}$ 　　 14. $\frac{12}{160}$ 　　 15. $\frac{6}{12}$ 　　 16. $\frac{16}{48}$

_____ 　　 _____ 　　 _____ 　　 _____

17. **Writing in Math** Explain how to tell $\frac{100}{105}$ is not in simplest form without finding all the factors.

_____

_____

_____

Test Prep Circle the correct letter for the answer.

18. A piece of property has been divided into lots. If Ray bought 4 lots, what part of the property did he buy?

    A $\frac{4}{7}$ 　　 B $\frac{3}{5}$ 　　 C $\frac{2}{3}$ 　　 D $\frac{1}{2}$

19. Which is $\frac{18}{40}$ in simplest form?

    A $\frac{9}{20}$ 　　 B $\frac{6}{15}$ 　　 C $\frac{7}{20}$ 　　 D $\frac{2}{3}$

Name _____

Math Diagnosis and Intervention System

Intervention Lesson **H18**

Using Number Sense to Compare Fractions

Example 1

When comparing two fractions with the same denominators, the fraction with the greater numerator is the greater fraction.

Compare $\frac{7}{8}$ and $\frac{5}{8}$. Write >, <, or =.

Step 1: Look at the denominators. Since they are the same, compare the numerators.

Step 2: Seven is greater than five, so $\frac{7}{8} > \frac{5}{8}$.

Example 2

Use fraction strips to show $\frac{2}{3}$ and $\frac{7}{9}$. Determine which is greater. Write > or <.

Step 1: Draw fraction strips to represent $\frac{2}{3}$ and $\frac{7}{9}$.

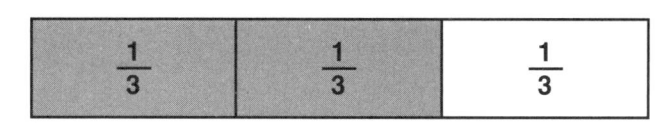

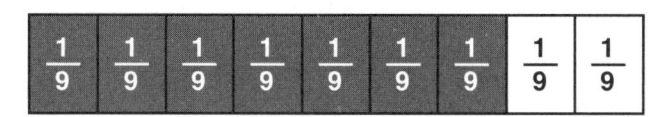

| $\frac{1}{3}$ | $\frac{1}{3}$ | $\frac{1}{3}$ |

| $\frac{1}{9}$ | $\frac{1}{9}$ | $\frac{1}{9}$ | $\frac{1}{9}$ | $\frac{1}{9}$ | $\frac{1}{9}$ | $\frac{1}{9}$ | $\frac{1}{9}$ | $\frac{1}{9}$ |

Step 2: Determine that $\frac{7}{9}$ is greater than $\frac{2}{3}$.

Step 3: Compare the fractions by stating $\frac{7}{9} > \frac{2}{3}$.

Write >, <, or = for each ◯. You may use fraction strips or drawings to help.

1. $\frac{3}{5}$ ◯ $\frac{1}{5}$
2. $\frac{5}{12}$ ◯ $\frac{7}{12}$
3. $\frac{3}{10}$ ◯ $\frac{9}{10}$
4. $\frac{3}{8}$ ◯ $\frac{5}{8}$

5. $\frac{3}{6}$ ◯ $\frac{4}{8}$
6. $\frac{2}{5}$ ◯ $\frac{1}{3}$
7. $\frac{5}{9}$ ◯ $\frac{4}{8}$
8. $\frac{3}{5}$ ◯ $\frac{2}{3}$

Intervention Lesson **H18**

Using Number Sense to Compare Fractions (continued)

Write >, <, or = for each ◯. You may use fraction strips or drawings to help.

9. $\dfrac{3}{7}$ ◯ $\dfrac{1}{7}$ 10. $\dfrac{5}{8}$ ◯ $\dfrac{10}{16}$ 11. $\dfrac{3}{11}$ ◯ $\dfrac{4}{10}$ 12. $\dfrac{3}{4}$ ◯ $\dfrac{2}{3}$

13. $\dfrac{3}{5}$ ◯ $\dfrac{9}{15}$ 14. $\dfrac{5}{6}$ ◯ $\dfrac{5}{8}$ 15. $\dfrac{5}{8}$ ◯ $\dfrac{7}{12}$ 16. $\dfrac{7}{9}$ ◯ $\dfrac{4}{9}$

Use the table for Questions 17–18.

Recipe	Amount of Sugar
Banana Bread	$\dfrac{2}{3}$ cup
Cinnamon Rolls	$\dfrac{1}{4}$ cup
Strawberry Delight	$\dfrac{1}{8}$ cup
Oatmeal Cookies	$\dfrac{3}{4}$ cup
Apricot Bars	$\dfrac{1}{2}$ cup

17. Which recipe uses more sugar, cinnamon rolls or oatmeal cookies? _____

18. Which recipe uses less sugar, apricot bars or banana bread? _____

19. **Reasoning** A pizza was cut into 8 pieces and you ate two. The same size pizza was cut into 12 pieces and your friend ate 3. Who ate more pizza, you or your friend? Explain.

_____

Test Prep Circle the correct letter for the answer.

20. Which fraction is greater than $\dfrac{3}{8}$?

   A $\dfrac{1}{8}$ **B** $\dfrac{4}{6}$ **C** $\dfrac{6}{16}$ **D** $\dfrac{3}{12}$

Comparing and Ordering Fractions

Intervention Lesson H19

Example

Compare: $\frac{4}{12} \bullet \frac{7}{9}$

Rewrite the fractions using the same denominator.
Think: What number has 12 and 9 as factors?

$$\frac{4}{12} = \frac{12}{36} \qquad \frac{7}{9} = \frac{28}{36}$$

Compare the new fractions: $\frac{12}{36} < \frac{28}{36}$

Write the comparison using the original fractions: $\frac{4}{12} < \frac{7}{9}$

Compare. Write >, <, or = for each ●.

1. $\frac{1}{4} \bullet \frac{3}{4}$ _____

2. $\frac{5}{10} \bullet \frac{3}{10}$ _____

3. $\frac{2}{3} \bullet \frac{5}{9}$ _____

4. $\frac{7}{9} \bullet \frac{28}{36}$ _____

5. $\frac{6}{15} \bullet \frac{2}{5}$ _____

6. $\frac{10}{14} \bullet \frac{4}{7}$ _____

7. $\frac{3}{5} \bullet \frac{7}{12}$ _____

8. $\frac{4}{14} \bullet \frac{2}{5}$ _____

9. $\frac{4}{7} \bullet \frac{2}{9}$ _____

10. $\frac{1}{5} \bullet \frac{2}{8}$ _____

11. $\frac{3}{8} \bullet \frac{2}{6}$ _____

12. $\frac{4}{6} \bullet \frac{5}{9}$ _____

Comparing and Ordering Fractions (continued)

Compare. Write >, <, or = for each ●.

13. $\frac{3}{5}$ ● $\frac{7}{15}$ _____
14. $\frac{8}{10}$ ● $\frac{13}{15}$ _____
15. $\frac{2}{8}$ ● $\frac{1}{4}$ _____
16. $\frac{7}{10}$ ● $\frac{3}{4}$ _____
17. $\frac{6}{14}$ ● $\frac{3}{7}$ _____
18. $\frac{8}{12}$ ● $\frac{5}{6}$ _____

Write each set of fractions in order from least to greatest.

19. $\frac{1}{4}, \frac{6}{7}, \frac{3}{5}$
20. $\frac{5}{8}, \frac{8}{10}, \frac{2}{7}$
21. $\frac{5}{9}, \frac{10}{12}, \frac{5}{7}$
22. $\frac{3}{9}, \frac{12}{15}, \frac{5}{6}$

_____ _____ _____ _____

23. **Math Reasoning** Give 3 fractions with different denominators that are less than $\frac{2}{3}$.

_____

24. Jim's height is 4 feet, $3\frac{3}{4}$ inches. Rex's height is 4 feet, $3\frac{3}{8}$ inches. Joan's height is 4 feet, $3\frac{7}{16}$ inches. Who is the tallest? Who is the shortest?

_____

25. Two students are writing stories. Eric's story is $\frac{2}{3}$ of a page. Jason's story is $\frac{5}{8}$ of a page. Whose story is longer?

_____

Test Prep Circle the correct letter for the answer.

26. Which fraction is greater than $\frac{5}{9}$?

   A $\frac{3}{6}$ **B** $\frac{1}{3}$ **C** $\frac{7}{18}$ **D** $\frac{2}{3}$

Name _____

Intervention Lesson **H20**

Math Diagnosis and Intervention System

Comparing and Ordering Fractions and Mixed Numbers

Example

Compare: $1\frac{4}{12}$ ● $1\frac{7}{9}$

Since the whole numbers are the same, compare the fractions.

Step 1
Find the LCM.   Multiples of 12: 12, 24, 36
                  Multiples of 9: 9, 18, 27, 36

The LCM is 36.

Step 2
Rewrite the fractions using the LCM as the new denominator.

$\frac{4}{12} = \frac{12}{36}$ $\frac{7}{9} = \frac{28}{36}$

Step 3
Compare the new fractions: $\frac{12}{36} < \frac{28}{36}$

Write the comparison using the original fractions: $1\frac{4}{12} < 1\frac{7}{9}$

Compare. Write >, <, or = for each ●.

1. $\frac{1}{4}$ ● $\frac{3}{8}$ _____

2. $\frac{5}{10}$ ● $\frac{3}{5}$ _____

3. $\frac{2}{3}$ ● $\frac{5}{9}$ _____

4. $\frac{7}{9}$ ● $\frac{28}{36}$ _____

5. $\frac{4}{15}$ ● $\frac{11}{5}$ _____

6. $4\frac{5}{15}$ ● $3\frac{4}{7}$ _____

7. $\frac{6}{5}$ ● $\frac{13}{12}$ _____

8. $3\frac{3}{4}$ ● $3\frac{2}{15}$ _____

9. $5\frac{4}{9}$ ● $5\frac{2}{7}$ _____

Intervention Lesson **H20**

Comparing and Ordering Fractions and Mixed Numbers (continued)

Compare. Write >, <, or = for each ●.

10. $\frac{3}{5}$ ● $\frac{7}{15}$ _____
11. $\frac{11}{10}$ ● $\frac{13}{15}$ _____
12. $3\frac{2}{8}$ ● $3\frac{1}{4}$ _____
13. $\frac{7}{10}$ ● $\frac{5}{4}$ _____
14. $\frac{6}{14}$ ● $\frac{5}{18}$ _____
15. $2\frac{8}{12}$ ● $2\frac{3}{4}$ _____

Write each set of fractions in order from least to greatest.

16. $\frac{1}{5}, \frac{6}{7}, \frac{3}{4}$
17. $\frac{9}{8}, \frac{8}{10}, \frac{9}{10}$
18. $\frac{14}{9}, \frac{10}{12}, \frac{5}{3}$
19. $1\frac{3}{7}, 1\frac{12}{15}, 1\frac{5}{6}$

_____ _____ _____ _____

20. **Mental Math** Which is bigger: $\frac{1}{4}$ or $\frac{1}{5}$? _____

21. Randy cut his pie into 8 pieces and ate 3. His sister cut her pie into 6 pieces and ate 1. They each gave a piece to 2 friends. Who ate more pie—Randy or his sister? _____

22. Two athletes are measuring how far they can jump. They each run 10 yards before their jump. Bill jumps 4 feet, $1\frac{3}{5}$ inches and Andy jumps 4 feet, $1\frac{5}{8}$ inches. Who jumped farther? _____

Test Prep Circle the correct letter for the answer.

23. Which fraction or mixed number is greater than $\frac{15}{9}$?

    A $1\frac{9}{18}$ B $1\frac{10}{18}$ C $\frac{15}{18}$ D $\frac{15}{6}$

24. Which comparison is correct?

    A $\frac{10}{11} > \frac{11}{10}$ B $\frac{10}{11} < \frac{11}{10}$ C $\frac{10}{11} = \frac{11}{10}$ D $\frac{10}{11} > 1\frac{1}{11}$

Intervention Lesson **H21**

Fractions and Division

Example

Find 12 ÷ 5.

Give the answer as a fraction, a mixed number, or a whole number.

12 ÷ 5 = $\frac{12}{5}$, or $2\frac{2}{5}$

Give each answer as a fraction, a mixed number, or a whole number.

1. 2 ÷ 6 = _____   **2.** 3 ÷ 2 = _____   **3.** 7 ÷ 9 = _____

4. 1 ÷ 5 = _____   **5.** 13 ÷ 2 = _____   **6.** 3 ÷ 4 = _____

7. 2 ÷ 8 = _____   **8.** 15 ÷ 3 = _____   **9.** 8 ÷ 9 = _____

10. 10 ÷ 4 = _____   **11.** 12 ÷ 3 = _____   **12.** 6 ÷ 8 = _____

13. 7 ÷ 10 = _____   **14.** 12 ÷ 11 = _____   **15.** 18 ÷ 6 = _____

16. 2 ÷ 5 = _____   **17.** 5 ÷ 2 = _____   **18.** 9 ÷ 13 = _____

Name _____

Intervention Lesson **H21**

Fractions and Division (continued)

Give each answer as a fraction, a mixed number, or a whole number.

19. $6 \div 2 =$ _____   **20.** $7 \div 2 =$ _____   **21.** $3 \div 9 =$ _____

22. $1 \div 4 =$ _____   **23.** $15 \div 2 =$ _____   **24.** $3 \div 5 =$ _____

25. Algebra Evaluate $x \div 3$ for $x = 7$. _____

26. Carlton has 3 apples to share between 4 friends. How much of an apple will each friend receive? _____

27. Mrs. Savage baked 5 apple pies and used 4 apples to make each pie. She is dividing the pies among 3 different dishes to give to friends. How much pie will be in each dish? _____

28. Eddie and 2 friends are cleaning the chalkboard for their teacher. Four other students are cleaning 5 erasers. How much of the chalkboard will each student clean? _____

Test Prep Circle the correct letter for the answer.

29. Find $16 \div 3$.

　A $\frac{3}{16}$　　**B** $5\frac{3}{1}$　　**C** $5\frac{1}{3}$　　**D** $4\frac{4}{3}$

30. Fred and Max are mowing 3 acres of land. How many acres will each boy mow?

　A $1\frac{1}{2}$　　**B** $\frac{2}{3}$　　**C** $\frac{5}{3}$　　**D** $\frac{3}{5}$

Intervention Lesson **H22**

Estimating Fractional Amounts

The fractions $\frac{1}{4}, \frac{1}{3}, \frac{1}{2}, \frac{2}{3}$, and $\frac{3}{4}$ can be used as **benchmark fractions** to **estimate** fractional amounts.

Example 1

About what fraction of the board is painted?

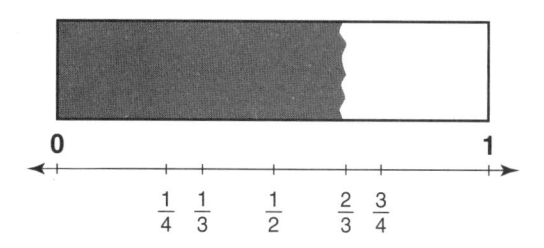

About $\frac{2}{3}$ of the board is painted.

Example 2

The school principal, Mr. Cardoza, found that 204 of the 590 students in Washington School were music students and that 303 students ride buses to school.

Mr. Cardoza wanted to report those facts to the school newspaper as fractions. How should he estimate the fraction of music students?

204 is about 200. 590 is about 600.

So, $\frac{204}{590}$ is about $\frac{200}{600}$. And $\frac{200}{600} = \frac{1}{3}$.

Mr. Cardoza reported that about $\frac{1}{3}$ of his students were music students.

For Questions 1–3, estimate the shaded part of each figure.

1.

2.

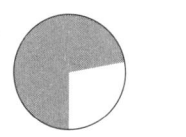

3.

4. See Example 2. About what fraction of Washington students ride buses?

Estimating Fractional Amounts (continued)

Estimate the shaded part of each.

5. _____

6. _____

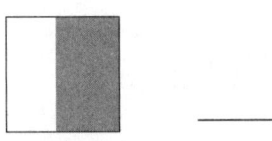

7. _____

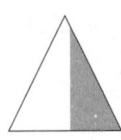

8. _____

Use the following table to answer Questions 9–11.

Number of Tiles in Students' Patriotic Mural	
Red	103
White	211
Blue	299

9. About what fraction of the tiles are blue? _____

10. About what fraction of the tiles are NOT blue? _____

11. About what fraction of the tiles are white? _____

12. **Number Sense** If about $\frac{1}{3}$ of an apple pie is gone, what part of the pie is left?

___

Test Prep Circle the correct letter for the answer.

13. What fraction of the figure is shaded?

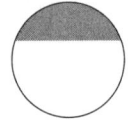

    A $\frac{1}{3}$ C $\frac{3}{4}$

    B $\frac{2}{3}$ D 1

44

Fractions and Mixed Numbers on the Number Line

Example

Points on a number line can represent fractions and mixed numbers. The length from 0 to 1 is divided into 10 equal parts. And the length from 1 to 2 is divided into 10 equal parts. The length of any one of the parts represents $\frac{1}{10}$.

```
        A                                    B
<---•---•---•---•---•---•---•---•---•---•---•---•---•---•---•---•---•---•---•---•--->
0   1/10 2/10 3/10 4/10 5/10 6/10 7/10 8/10 9/10  1  11/10 12/10 13/10 14/10 15/10 16/10 17/10 18/10 19/10  2
```

What fractions represent point A and point B?

Point A is located at three equal parts from zero. So, $\frac{3}{10}$ represents point A.

Point B can be shown as an improper fraction and a mixed number.

It is 15 equal parts from the zero. It is also 1 whole and 5 equal parts from zero.

So, point B can be represented by both $\frac{15}{10}$ and $1\frac{5}{10}$.

What fraction or mixed number represents each point?

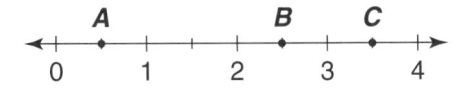

```
   A       B   C
<--•---•---•---•---•-->
0   1   2   3   4
```

1. Point A _____ **2.** Point B _____ **3.** Point C _____

```
  D    E    F
<-•-•--•-•--•-•-•->
0      1       2
```

4. Point D _____ **5.** Point E _____ **6.** Point F _____

45

Fractions and Mixed Numbers on the Number Line (continued)

What number represents each point? If a point can be represented by both an improper fraction and a mixed number, give both.

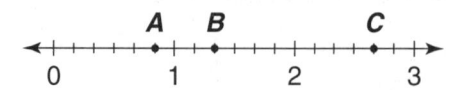

```
      A   B       C
<--+-+-•-+-•-+-+-+-+-•-+-+->
   0   1   2   3
```

7. Point A _____ **8.** Point B _____ **9.** Point C _____

```
        D     E    F
<--+-+-•-+-+-•-+-+-•-+-+->
   0     1     2
```

10. Point D _____ **11.** Point E _____ **12.** Point F _____

Draw a number line to show each set of numbers. Then order the numbers from least to greatest.

13. $\frac{2}{8}, 1\frac{3}{8}, \frac{10}{8}$

14. $\frac{3}{8}, \frac{14}{8}, \frac{1}{2}$

_____ _____

15. $\frac{7}{9}, \frac{2}{9}, \frac{12}{9}$

16. $1\frac{4}{8}, 1\frac{1}{8}, \frac{13}{8}$

_____ _____

17. Writing in Math If the numerator is greater than the denominator, is the fraction less than 1 or greater than 1? Explain.

_____

_____

_____

Test Prep Circle the correct letter for the answer.

18. What fraction or mixed number is represented by point W?

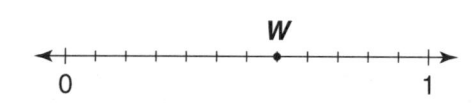

```
                        W
         <--+-+-+-+-+-+-+-•-+-+-+->
            0                     1
```

A $\frac{6}{12}$ **B** $1\frac{1}{12}$ **C** $\frac{7}{12}$ **D** $\frac{5}{12}$

46

Name _____

Intervention Lesson **H24**

Math Diagnosis and Intervention System

Equivalent Fractions

Example 1

Use multiplication to find a fraction that is equivalent to $\frac{3}{7}$.

Multiply the numerator and denominator by the same number.

$3 \longrightarrow \times 2 = 6$
$7 \longrightarrow \times 2 = 14$

Example 2

Use division to write a fraction that is equivalent to $\frac{16}{20}$.

Think of a number that is a factor of both 16 and 20.

2 is a factor of both 16 and 20.
Divide the numerator and denominator by that factor.

$16 \div 2 = 8$
$20 \div 2 = 10$

If you continue to divide until 1 is the only factor of both the numerator and the denominator, you find the fraction in simplest form.

$16 \div 2 = 8 \div 2 = 4$
$20 \div 2 = 10 \div 2 = 5$

$\frac{8}{10}$ and $\frac{4}{5}$ are both equivalent to $\frac{16}{20}$. Only $\frac{4}{5}$ is in simplest form.

---

1. $\frac{1}{4} = \frac{}{8}$

2. $\frac{5}{10} = \frac{}{2}$

3. $\frac{2}{3} = \frac{}{9}$

4. $\frac{7}{9} = \frac{}{36}$

5. $\frac{6}{15} = \frac{}{5}$

6. $\frac{18}{24} = \frac{}{4}$

7. $\frac{5}{3} = \frac{}{12}$

8. $\frac{12}{20} = \frac{}{5}$

9. $\frac{4}{7} = \frac{}{21}$

47

Name _____

Intervention Lesson **H24**

Math Diagnosis and Intervention System

Equivalent Fractions (continued)

10. $\dfrac{1}{5} = \dfrac{}{15}$

11. $\dfrac{8}{10} = \dfrac{}{5}$

12. $\dfrac{2}{8} = \dfrac{}{4}$

13. $\dfrac{7}{10} = \dfrac{}{20}$

14. $\dfrac{6}{14} = \dfrac{}{7}$

15. $\dfrac{8}{11} = \dfrac{}{22}$

Write a fraction or mixed number equivalent to the fraction shown.

16. $\dfrac{3}{7}$ _____

17. $\dfrac{1}{8}$ _____

18. $2\dfrac{3}{5}$ _____

19. $\dfrac{6}{10}$ _____

Write each fraction or mixed number in simplest form.

20. $\dfrac{9}{12}$ _____

21. $\dfrac{10}{15}$ _____

22. $1\dfrac{6}{8}$ _____

23. $\dfrac{16}{24}$ _____

24. **Math Reasoning** Use 2 number lines to show that $\dfrac{1}{3}$ is the same as $\dfrac{2}{6}$.

25. On Tuesday, $\dfrac{2}{3}$ of the class time was spent on English projects. Write three equivalent fractions for $\dfrac{2}{3}$. _____

Test Prep Circle the correct letter for the answer.

26. Which fraction is equivalent to $\dfrac{5}{9}$?

    A $\dfrac{10}{9}$
    B $\dfrac{10}{18}$
    C $\dfrac{15}{18}$
    D $\dfrac{5}{18}$

27. Which fraction is in simplest form?

    A $\dfrac{5}{6}$
    B $\dfrac{4}{6}$
    C $\dfrac{3}{6}$
    D $\dfrac{2}{6}$

Name _____

Math Diagnosis and Intervention System

Intervention Lesson **H25**

Relating Fractions and Decimals

Example

Write a fraction and a decimal for the shaded parts of the set.

$\frac{2}{5}$ of the shapes are shaded.

$\frac{2}{5} = 2 \div 5 = 0.4 \qquad 5\overline{)2.0}^{\,0.4}$

Write a fraction and a decimal for each shaded part.

1.

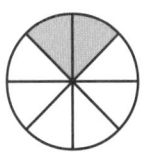

2.

3.

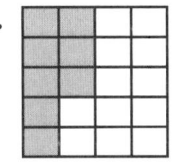

4.

5.

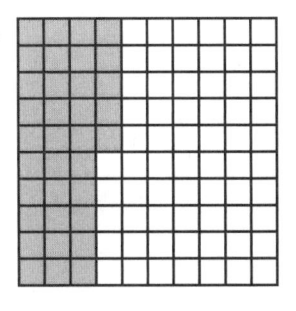

6.

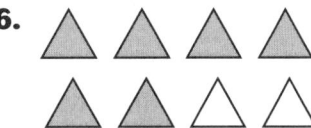

49

Name _____

Intervention Lesson **H25**

Relating Fractions and Decimals (continued)

Write a fraction and a decimal for each shaded part.

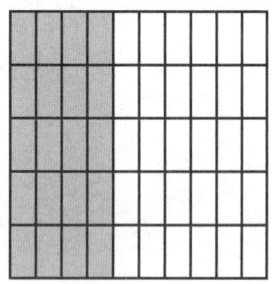

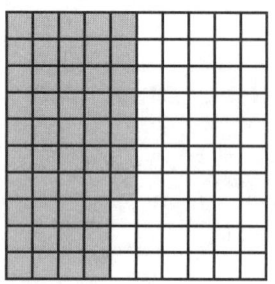

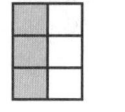

7. _____

8. _____

9. _____

10. _____

Use the number line to write a fraction and a decimal for each point.

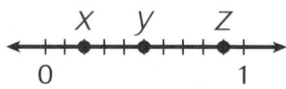

11. Point X

12. Point Y

13. Point Z

_____   _____   _____

14. Math Reasoning Write $\frac{1}{4}$ as a decimal. What is $\frac{1}{4}$ of a dollar? How are these two numbers related?

_____

15. Mary has 6 stuffed animals. Three of them are bears and 2 of them are rabbits. Write a fraction and a decimal to represent the bears. _____

Test Prep Circle the correct letter for the answer.

16. Find the decimal that is the same as $\frac{12}{50}$.

  A 0.12   **B** 0.06   **C** 0.24   **D** 0.50

Name _____

Intervention Lesson **H26**

Fractions, Decimals, and the Number Line

Example 1

Show 4.3 on a number line.

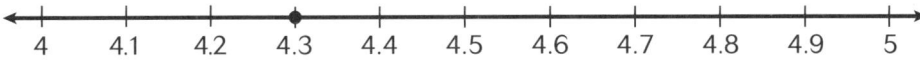

```
←—+—+—+—•—+—+—+—+—+—+—→
  4  4.1 4.2 4.3 4.4 4.5 4.6 4.7 4.8 4.9  5
```

Place 4 and 5 on a number line.
Then divide the distance from
4 to 5 into 10 equal parts.

Example 2

Which point is located at 8.63?

8.63 is not quite halfway
between 8.60 and 8.70.

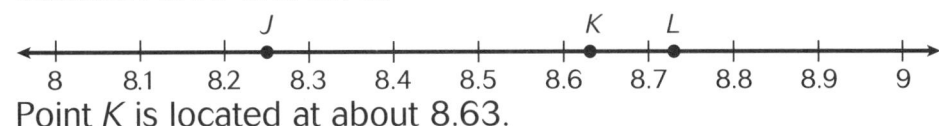

```
                 J              K   L
←—+—+—•—+—+—+—•—•—+—+—→
  8  8.1 8.2 8.3 8.4 8.5 8.6 8.7 8.8 8.9  9
```

Point K is located at about 8.63.

For Exercises 1–6, use the two number lines below. What point shows the location of each number?

1. 9.3   **2.** 9.61   **3.** $9\frac{1}{10}$ **4.** 1.8   **5.** $1\frac{16}{100}$ **6.** 1.48

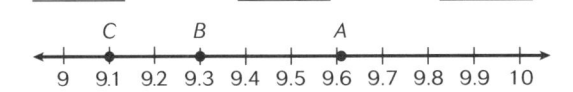

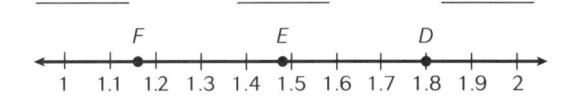

```
        C   B       A                              F       E       D
←—+—•—+—•—+—+—+—•—+—+—+—→     ←—+—+—•—+—+—+—•—+—+—•—+—→
  9  9.1 9.2 9.3 9.4 9.5 9.6 9.7 9.8 9.9 10       1 1.1 1.2 1.3 1.4 1.5 1.6 1.7 1.8 1.9 2
```

For Exercises 7–12, use the two number lines below. What point shows the location of each number?

7. 6.0   **8.** $6\frac{1}{2}$ **9.** 6.87   **10.** 3.7   **11.** 3.78   **12.** $3\frac{3}{4}$

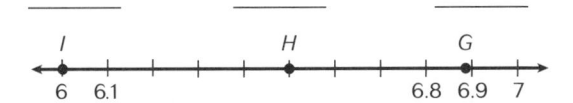

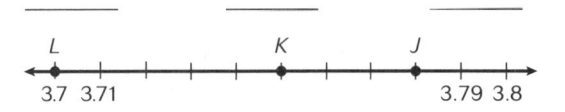

```
   I              H           G                     L                 K                 J
←—•—+—+—+—+—+—+—+—•—+—+—•—+—→     ←—•—+—+—+—+—+—+—•—+—+—+—•—+—→
  6  6.1                  6.8 6.9  7               3.7 3.71                                    3.79 3.8
```

51

Name _____

Math Diagnosis and Intervention System

Intervention Lesson **H26**

Fractions, Decimals, and the Number Line (continued)

For Exercises 13–18, use the two number lines below. What point shows the location of each number?

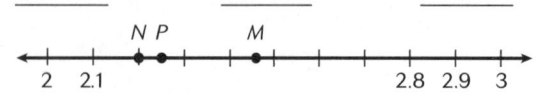

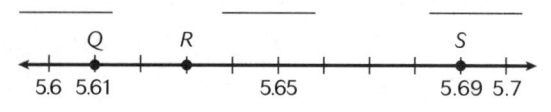

13. 2.2   **14.** 2.46   **15.** $2\frac{1}{4}$ **16.** 5.69   **17.** 5.63   **18.** 5.61

```
        N P      M                          Q      R                    S
  ←──●─●──┼──●──┼──┼──●──●──→    ←──┼──●──┼──┼──┼──┼──●──┼──→
     2  2.1              2.8 2.9 3         5.6 5.61       5.65        5.69 5.7
```

Show each set of numbers on a number line. Then order the numbers from least to greatest.

19. $5\frac{1}{2}$, 6.8, $6\frac{3}{10}$

_____

20. $\frac{18}{4}$, 4.73, 4.1

_____

21. 8.12, $8\frac{3}{5}$, 8.87

_____

22. The kids in Room 8 measured their feet. Brandon's foot is $7\frac{1}{4}$ inches long, Jenny's is 7.4 inches, Brenda's is $6\frac{4}{5}$ inches. Show these numbers on a number line. Whose foot is the shortest? _____

Test Prep Circle the correct letter for the answer.

23. What point is shown on the number line?

```
  ←──┼──●──┼──┼──┼──┼──┼──┼──┼──→
     5                          6
```

A 5.35   **B** 5.2   **C** 5.25   **D** 5.3

24. What point is shown on the number line?

```
  ←──┼──┼──┼──┼──┼──●──┼──┼──→
     7.3                  7.4
```

A 7.36   **B** 7.37   **C** 7.3   **D** 7.38

52

Name _____

Math Diagnosis and Intervention System

Intervention Lesson **H27**

Adding and Subtracting Fractions

Example

Find $\frac{2}{5} + \frac{1}{5}$.

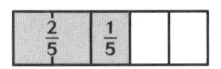

$\frac{2}{5} + \frac{1}{5} = \frac{3}{5}$ ← add the numerators
← use the same denominator

Find each sum or difference. You may use fraction strips to help.

1. $\frac{1}{3} + \frac{1}{3} =$ _____

2. $\frac{1}{5} + \frac{3}{5} =$ _____

3. $\frac{1}{4} + \frac{2}{4} =$ _____

4. $\frac{5}{6} - \frac{3}{6} =$ _____

5. $\frac{3}{5} - \frac{1}{5} =$ _____

6. $\frac{3}{7} + \frac{2}{7} =$ _____

53

Name _____

Intervention Lesson **H27**

Adding and Subtracting Fractions (continued)

Find each sum or difference. You may use fraction strips to help.

7. $\frac{3}{4} - \frac{1}{4} = $ _____

8. $\frac{2}{6} + \frac{3}{6} = $ _____

9. $\frac{4}{5} - \frac{2}{5} = $ _____

10. $\frac{2}{8} + \frac{5}{8} = $ _____

11. $\frac{4}{7} - \frac{3}{7} = $ _____

12. $\frac{7}{8} - \frac{1}{8} = $ _____

13. **Algebra** What fraction would you add to $\frac{1}{3}$ to get $\frac{3}{3}$? _____

14. Calvin bought a gallon of ice cream. He ate $\frac{1}{6}$ of it the first day, and he ate $\frac{2}{6}$ of it the second day. What fraction of the ice cream did he eat? _____

15. Three-fifths of Mr. James' class are wearing blue jeans and white shirts. One-fifth of the students are wearing blue jeans and red shirts. One-fifth are wearing brown pants and white shirts. What fraction of Mr. James' class are wearing white shirts? _____

Test Prep Circle the correct letter for the answer.

16. Find $\frac{5}{6} - \frac{1}{6}$.

    A $\frac{6}{6}$ B $\frac{5}{6}$ C $\frac{4}{6}$ D $\frac{6}{4}$

17. Bill has $\frac{1}{4}$ of a bag of pretzels, and Phillip has $\frac{2}{4}$ of a bag. What fraction of a bag of pretzels do they have together?

    A $\frac{2}{8}$ B $\frac{3}{4}$ C $\frac{1}{4}$ D $\frac{4}{3}$

Name _____

Intervention Lesson **H28**

Math Diagnosis and Intervention System

Estimating Fraction Sums and Differences

Example 1

You can use fraction strips to estimate fraction sums.

Compare: $\frac{4}{5} + \frac{3}{10}$ ◯ 1

$\frac{4}{5} + \frac{3}{10} > 1$

The denominators are different.

Use fraction strips to find equivalent fractions with the same denominators.

Example 2

You can use fraction strips to estimate fraction differences.

Compare: $\frac{5}{8} - \frac{3}{8}$ ◯ $\frac{1}{2}$

$\frac{5}{8} - \frac{3}{8} < \frac{1}{2}$

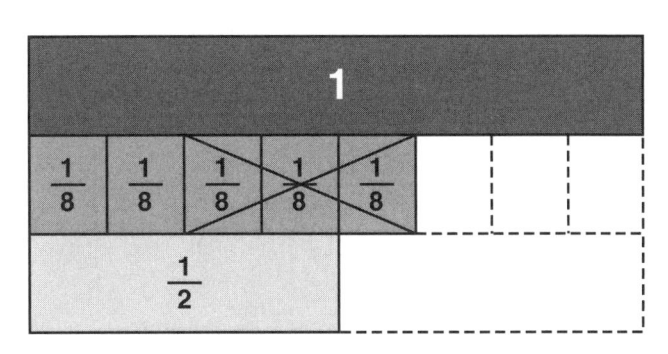

Use fraction strips to show each problem. Write > or < for each ◯.

1. $\frac{1}{2} + \frac{3}{4}$ ◯ 1
2. $\frac{3}{4} - \frac{1}{3}$ ◯ $\frac{1}{2}$
3. $\frac{5}{6} + \frac{2}{3}$ ◯ 1
4. $\frac{9}{10} - \frac{1}{10}$ ◯ $\frac{1}{2}$
5. $\frac{2}{5} + \frac{1}{5}$ ◯ 1
6. $\frac{7}{12} - \frac{1}{4}$ ◯ $\frac{1}{2}$

55

Name _____

Math Diagnosis and Intervention System

Intervention Lesson **H28**

Estimating Fraction Sums and Differences (continued)

Use fraction strips to show each problem. Write > or < for each ◯.

7. $\frac{3}{8} - \frac{1}{4}$ ◯ $\frac{1}{2}$ 　　　 8. $\frac{3}{5} + \frac{1}{10}$ ◯ 1 　　　 9. $\frac{7}{12} - \frac{1}{3}$ ◯ $\frac{1}{2}$

10. $\frac{1}{6} + \frac{7}{8}$ ◯ 1 　　　 11. $\frac{1}{4} - \frac{1}{8}$ ◯ $\frac{1}{2}$ 　　　 12. $\frac{1}{2} + \frac{7}{12}$ ◯ 1

13. $\frac{3}{10} - \frac{1}{5}$ ◯ $\frac{1}{2}$ 　　　 14. $\frac{5}{6} + \frac{1}{2}$ ◯ 1 　　　 15. $\frac{1}{2} - \frac{1}{12}$ ◯ $\frac{1}{2}$

Solve.

16. Is one quarter-hour plus one quarter-hour more or less than 1 hour?

    _____

17. Is 1 hour minus one quarter-hour more or less than one half-hour?

    _____

18. Is the sum of $\frac{1}{2} + \frac{3}{4}$ more or less than 1?

    _____

19. Is the difference between $\frac{9}{10} - \frac{1}{5}$ more or less than $\frac{1}{2}$?

    _____

20. **Number Sense** When you add two fractions that are each greater than $\frac{1}{2}$, is the sum less than or greater than 1?

    _____

Test Prep Circle the correct letter for the answer.

21. $\frac{3}{4} + \frac{1}{2}$ ◯ 1

    A　<　　　　B　−　　　　C　+　　　　D　>

22. $\frac{7}{8} - \frac{5}{8}$ ◯ $\frac{1}{2}$

    A　<　　　　B　−　　　　C　+　　　　D　>

56

Name _____

Intervention Lesson **H29**

Math Diagnosis and Intervention System

Adding and Subtracting Fractions with Like Denominators

Example

Find $\frac{2}{5} + \frac{1}{5}$.

$\frac{2}{5} + \frac{1}{5} = \frac{3}{5}$ ← add the numerators
← use the same denominator

Find each sum or difference. You may use fraction strips to help.

1. $\frac{1}{3} + \frac{1}{3} =$ _____

2. $\frac{1}{5} + \frac{3}{5} =$ _____

3. $\frac{1}{4} + \frac{2}{4} =$ _____

4. $\frac{5}{6} - \frac{3}{6} =$ _____

5. $\frac{3}{5} - \frac{1}{5} =$ _____

6. $\frac{3}{7} + \frac{2}{7} =$ _____

Name _____

Intervention Lesson **H29**

Adding and Subtracting Fractions with Like Denominators (continued)

Find each sum or difference. You may use fraction strips to help.

7. $\frac{3}{4} - \frac{1}{4} =$ _____

8. $\frac{2}{6} + \frac{3}{6} =$ _____

9. $\frac{4}{5} - \frac{2}{5} =$ _____

10. $\frac{2}{8} + \frac{5}{8} =$ _____

11. $\frac{4}{7} - \frac{3}{7} =$ _____

12. $\frac{7}{8} - \frac{1}{8} =$ _____

13. **Algebra** What fraction would you add to $\frac{1}{3}$ to get $\frac{3}{3}$? _____

14. Calvin bought a gallon of ice cream. He ate $\frac{1}{6}$ of it the first day and he ate $\frac{2}{6}$ of it the second day. What fraction of the ice cream did he eat? _____

15. Three-fifths of Mr. James' class are wearing blue jeans and white shirts. One-fifth of the students are wearing blue jeans and red shirts. One-fifth are wearing brown pants and white shirts. What fraction of Mr. James' class are wearing white shirts? _____

Test Prep Circle the correct letter for the answer.

16. Find $\frac{5}{6} - \frac{1}{6}$.

    A $\frac{6}{6}$ B $\frac{5}{6}$ C $\frac{4}{6}$ D $\frac{6}{4}$

17. Bill has $\frac{1}{4}$ of a bag of pretzels and Phillip has $\frac{2}{4}$ of a bag. What fraction of a bag of pretzels do they have together?

    A $\frac{2}{8}$ B $\frac{3}{4}$ C $\frac{1}{4}$ D $\frac{4}{3}$

Intervention Lesson **H30**

Least Common Denominator

Example

The **least common denominator (LCD)** of two fractions is the **least common multiple (LCM)** of their denominators.

Find the least common denominator (LCD) of $\frac{1}{6}$ and $\frac{3}{8}$.

List the first several multiples of 6: 6, 12, 18, **24**, 30, 36, 42, **48**, 54, 60

List the first several multiples of 8: 8, 16, **24**, 32, 40, **48**, 56

The common multiple of 6 and 8 in the lists above are 24 and 48. The smaller of those two numbers, 24, is the least common multiple (LCM) of 6 and 8.

So, 24 is the least common denominator (LCD) of $\frac{1}{6}$ and $\frac{3}{8}$.

Find the least common multiple (LCM) for each pair of numbers.

1. 4 and 8   **2.** 8 and 12   **3.** 6 and 12

_____   _____   _____

4. 12 and 18   **5.** 7 and 9   **6.** 10 and 4

_____   _____   _____

7. 8 and 10   **8.** 5 and 12   **9.** 9 and 5

_____   _____   _____

10. 10 and 15   **11.** 15 and 20   **12.** 8 and 20

_____   _____   _____

Name _____

Intervention Lesson **H30**

Least Common Denominator (continued)

Find the least common denominator (LCD) for each pair of fractions.

13. $\frac{1}{6}$ and $\frac{2}{3}$ _____   14. $\frac{5}{8}$ and $\frac{3}{16}$ _____   15. $\frac{1}{3}$ and $\frac{1}{9}$ _____

16. $\frac{7}{10}$ and $\frac{2}{5}$ _____   17. $\frac{3}{4}$ and $\frac{5}{16}$ _____   18. $\frac{3}{12}$ and $\frac{1}{2}$ _____

19. $\frac{2}{3}$ and $\frac{3}{8}$ _____   20. $\frac{7}{20}$ and $\frac{1}{4}$ _____   21. $\frac{1}{4}$ and $\frac{1}{6}$ _____

22. $\frac{2}{15}$ and $\frac{1}{30}$ _____   23. $\frac{3}{7}$ and $\frac{4}{5}$ _____   24. $\frac{1}{5}$ and $\frac{2}{3}$ _____

25. A car travels $\frac{1}{4}$ of a mile and stops. It then travels $\frac{3}{8}$ of a mile farther before stopping again. What is the least common denominator (LCD) for the fractions? _____

26. **Writing in Math** Because 5 × 10 = 50, we know that 50 is a common multiple of 5 and 10. Is it the least common multiple of 5 and 10? Explain.

_____

_____

27. **Mental Math** Find the least common multiple for 6 and 10.

_____

Test Prep Circle the correct letter for the answer.

28. What is the least common denominator for $\frac{7}{8}$ and $\frac{1}{5}$?

   A 16   **B** 20   **C** 35   **D** 40

29. Find the least common multiple of 6 and 14.

   A 14   **B** 24   **C** 42   **D** 84

60

Name _____

Math Diagnosis and Intervention System

Intervention Lesson **H31**

Adding and Subtracting Fractions with Unlike Denominators

Example

Find $\frac{1}{3} + \frac{1}{6}$.

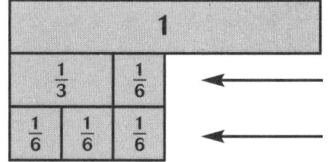

← The denominators are different.

← Use fraction strips to find equivalent fractions with the same denominators.

$\frac{2}{6} + \frac{1}{6} = \frac{3}{6}$

Find each sum or difference. You may use fraction strips to help.

1. $\frac{2}{3} + \frac{1}{6} =$ _____
2. $\frac{1}{5} + \frac{3}{10} =$ _____
3. $\frac{3}{8} + \frac{2}{4} =$ _____

4. $\frac{5}{6} - \frac{2}{3} =$ _____
5. $\frac{3}{5} - \frac{1}{10} =$ _____
6. $\frac{3}{4} - \frac{1}{2} =$ _____

7. $\frac{3}{4} + \frac{2}{8} =$ _____
8. $\frac{1}{2} - \frac{1}{4} =$ _____
9. $\frac{1}{6} + \frac{5}{12} =$ _____

10. $\frac{1}{8} + \frac{1}{2} =$ _____
11. $\frac{2}{3} - \frac{2}{12} =$ _____
12. $\frac{1}{2} - \frac{2}{4} =$ _____

13. $\frac{3}{4} - \frac{3}{8} =$ _____
14. $\frac{1}{4} + \frac{4}{8} =$ _____
15. $\frac{2}{3} + \frac{2}{6} =$ _____

Intervention Lesson **H31**

Adding and Subtracting Fractions with Unlike Denominators (continued)

Find each sum or difference. You may use fraction strips to help.

16. $\dfrac{3}{4} - \dfrac{1}{8} =$ _____

17. $\dfrac{2}{6} + \dfrac{1}{3} =$ _____

18. $\dfrac{4}{5} - \dfrac{2}{10} =$ _____

19. $\dfrac{2}{4} + \dfrac{1}{8} =$ _____

20. $\dfrac{4}{6} - \dfrac{3}{12} =$ _____

21. $\dfrac{7}{8} - \dfrac{1}{2} =$ _____

22. $\dfrac{3}{4} - \dfrac{2}{8} =$ _____

23. $\dfrac{4}{6} - \dfrac{1}{3} =$ _____

24. $\dfrac{3}{8} + \dfrac{1}{2} =$ _____

25. **Math Reasoning** Find 3 fractions that are equivalent to $\dfrac{1}{2}$.

_____

26. Renee watched $\dfrac{2}{3}$ of the movie and Timothy watched $\dfrac{3}{6}$ of the movie. How much more did Renee watch than Timothy? _____

27. A jar is filled with red, blue, and green marbles. Half of the marbles are red. One-third of the marbles are blue. One-sixth of the marbles are green. What fraction of the marbles are either red or blue? _____

Test Prep Circle the correct letter for the answer.

28. Find $\dfrac{5}{6} - \dfrac{1}{12}$.

  A $\dfrac{4}{6}$ B $\dfrac{9}{12}$ C $\dfrac{4}{12}$ D $\dfrac{3}{6}$

29. Rick and Laura are painting a fence. Rick has painted $\dfrac{3}{8}$ of the fence and Laura has painted $\dfrac{1}{4}$. How much of the fence have Laura and Rick painted?

  A $\dfrac{0}{8}$ B $\dfrac{3}{4}$ C $\dfrac{3}{6}$ D $\dfrac{5}{8}$

Name _____

Math Diagnosis and Intervention System

Intervention Lesson **H32**

Investigating Adding and Subtracting Mixed Numbers

You need a ruler for this lesson.

Example 1

Find $1\frac{3}{8} + 1\frac{7}{8}$. Draw a line $1\frac{3}{8}$ inches long.

Starting at one end, continue drawing the line for $1\frac{7}{8}$ inches more.

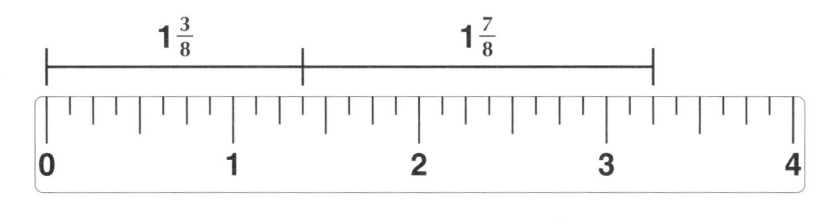

Then measure the line. Its length is $3\frac{2}{8}$ inches, or $3\frac{1}{4}$ inches.

So, $1\frac{3}{8} + 1\frac{7}{8} = 3\frac{2}{8}$, or $3\frac{1}{4}$.

Example 2

You can also use a ruler to subtract $3\frac{1}{8} - 1\frac{1}{2}$.

Draw a line $3\frac{1}{8}$ inches long. Mark $1\frac{1}{2}$ inches along the line.

The line is now marked into two parts. One part is $1\frac{1}{2}$ inches.

Measure the other part. It is $1\frac{5}{8}$ inches.

So, $3\frac{1}{8} - 1\frac{1}{2} = 1\frac{5}{8}$.

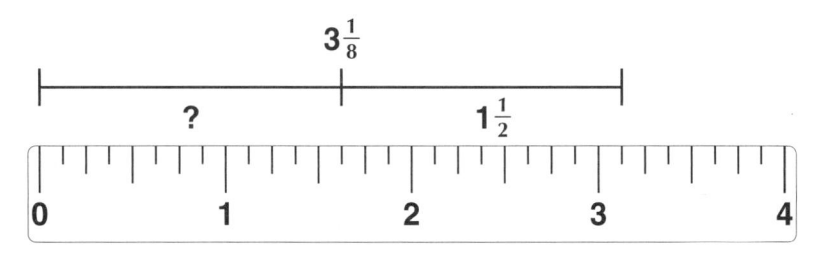

Find each sum or difference. Simplify the answer, if necessary.
You may use fraction strips or draw pictures to help.

1. $1\frac{3}{4} + 1\frac{3}{4}$

2. $2\frac{5}{8} + 1\frac{7}{8}$

63

Math Diagnosis and Intervention System

Intervention Lesson **H32**

Name _____

Investigating Adding and Subtracting Mixed Numbers (continued)

Find each sum or difference. Simplify the answer, if necessary.
You may use fraction strips or a ruler to help.

3. $1\frac{1}{4} + 2\frac{1}{4}$

4. $3\frac{1}{8} + 3\frac{7}{8}$

5. $5\frac{3}{8} + 4\frac{7}{8}$

_____   _____   _____

6. $3\frac{1}{4} - 1\frac{1}{2}$

7. $4\frac{5}{8} - 3\frac{6}{8}$

8. $3\frac{1}{2} - 1\frac{5}{8}$

_____   _____   _____

9. $3\frac{1}{8} + 4\frac{5}{8}$

10. $3\frac{4}{8} - 1\frac{5}{8}$

11. $8\frac{1}{2} + 6\frac{1}{2}$

_____   _____   _____

12. Ms. Sweeny is baking muffins and a cake. The muffin recipe calls for $2\frac{1}{4}$ cups of flour. The cake recipe calls for $3\frac{1}{4}$ cups of flour. How much flour does she need to make both recipes? _____

13. This week, Martin spent $1\frac{5}{8}$ hours playing soccer and $4\frac{1}{8}$ hours doing homework. How much longer did he spend doing homework than playing soccer? _____

14. **Mental Math** How many fourths are in $2\frac{1}{4}$? _____

Test Prep Circle the correct letter for the answer.

15. Find $2\frac{3}{4} + 4\frac{1}{4}$.

    A 9   **B** $8\frac{1}{4}$ **C** 7   **D** $6\frac{1}{4}$

16. From Kevin's house to school is $3\frac{1}{2}$ miles. How far is a round trip?

    A 6 miles   **B** $6\frac{1}{2}$ miles   **C** 7 miles   **D** 8 miles

64

Name _____

Intervention Lesson **H33**

Estimating Sums and Differences of Mixed Numbers

Example

Estimate $4\frac{1}{3} - 1\frac{2}{3}$.

You can estimate sums and differences of mixed numbers by rounding each number to the nearest whole number. If the fraction is greater than or equal to $\frac{1}{2}$, round up to the next whole number. Otherwise, round down.

$4\frac{1}{3} \longrightarrow 4 \qquad \frac{1}{3} < \frac{1}{2}$ so round to 4

$-1\frac{2}{3} \longrightarrow -2 \qquad \frac{2}{3} > \frac{1}{2}$ so round to 2

The answer is about 2.

Estimate each sum or difference.

1. $2\frac{2}{3}$
   $-1\frac{1}{3}$

2. $\frac{4}{5}$
   $+\frac{3}{5}$

3. $5\frac{1}{4}$
   $-\frac{2}{4}$

4. $6\frac{4}{6}$
   $+1\frac{5}{6}$

5. $6\frac{7}{8}$
   $-5\frac{3}{8}$

6. 6
   $-3\frac{3}{9}$

7. $4\frac{9}{14}$
   $+2\frac{11}{14}$

8. 6
   $+4\frac{2}{16}$

9. $2\frac{9}{10}$
   $-1\frac{5}{10}$

10. 5
    $+4\frac{2}{4}$

11. $2\frac{2}{9}$
    $+3\frac{2}{9}$

12. $4\frac{1}{5}$
    $-\frac{3}{5}$

65

Math Diagnosis and Intervention System

Intervention Lesson **H33**

Name _____

Estimating Sums and Differences of Mixed Numbers (continued)

Estimate each sum or difference.

13. $2\frac{9}{10}$
    $+ 1\frac{1}{10}$
    _____

    _____

14. $5\frac{1}{4}$
    $+ 4\frac{2}{4}$
    _____

    _____

15. $3\frac{2}{9}$
    $- \frac{2}{9}$
    _____

    _____

16. $4\frac{4}{5}$
    $+ \frac{3}{5}$
    _____

    _____

17. $2\frac{3}{4} - 1 = $ _____

    _____

18. $7\frac{2}{6} + 6\frac{5}{6} = $ _____

    _____

19. $3\frac{2}{5} + 1\frac{2}{5} = $ _____

    _____

20. $6\frac{1}{8} - 1\frac{5}{8} = $ _____

    _____

21. $7 - 2\frac{3}{7} = $ _____

    _____

22. $3\frac{4}{8} + 1\frac{7}{8} = $ _____

    _____

23. **Algebra** Estimate the solution: $n + 1\frac{1}{8} = 7\frac{5}{8}$ _____

24. Yolanda walked $2\frac{3}{5}$ miles on Monday, $1\frac{1}{5}$ miles on Tuesday, and $3\frac{4}{5}$ miles on Wednesday. Estimate how far she walked on all three days. _____

25. Chris is going to add $2\frac{1}{4}$ cups of a chemical to the swimming pool when he finds out that Richard has already added $1\frac{1}{8}$ cups of the chemical. Estimate how much more Chris should add so that the total is his original amount. _____

Test Prep Circle the correct letter for the answer.

26. Estimate $4\frac{2}{6} - 1\frac{5}{6}$.

    A 4   **B** 3   **C** 2   **D** 1

Name _____

Intervention Lesson **H34**

Adding Mixed Numbers

Example

Find $1\frac{3}{6} + 3\frac{5}{8}$.

Step 1 Find LCD.

$$1\frac{3}{6} = 1\frac{}{24}$$
$$+ 3\frac{5}{8} = 3\frac{}{24}$$

Step 2 Write equivalent fractions using the LCD.

$$1\frac{3}{6} = 1\frac{12}{24}$$
$$+ 3\frac{5}{8} = 3\frac{15}{24}$$

Step 3 Add. Simplify if possible.

$$1\frac{12}{24}$$
$$+ 3\frac{15}{24}$$
$$4\frac{27}{24} = 5\frac{3}{24} = 5\frac{1}{8}$$

Estimate to check.
$2 + 4 = 6$

Add. Simplify, if possible. Estimate to check.

1. $2\frac{1}{2}$
$+ 1\frac{1}{3}$

2. $1\frac{1}{5}$
$+ 3\frac{3}{10}$

3. $1\frac{3}{4}$
$+ \frac{2}{5}$

4. $2\frac{5}{12}$
$+ 3\frac{5}{6}$

_____ _____ _____ _____

5. $6\frac{5}{6}$
$+ 5\frac{3}{8}$

6. $6\frac{1}{9}$
$+ 3\frac{2}{3}$

7. $4\frac{3}{4}$
$+ 7\frac{5}{6}$

8. $6\frac{1}{16}$
$+ 4\frac{3}{8}$

_____ _____ _____ _____

67

Math Diagnosis and Intervention System

Intervention Lesson **H34**

Name _____

Adding Mixed Numbers (continued)

Add. Simplify, if possible. Estimate to check.

9. $2\frac{1}{5}$
  $+ 1\frac{7}{10}$
  _____

10. $4\frac{3}{8}$
  $+ \frac{3}{4}$
  _____

11. $2\frac{5}{6}$
  $+ 2\frac{4}{9}$
  _____

12. $4\frac{4}{5}$
  $+ \frac{1}{2}$
  _____

13. $2\frac{3}{4} + 7\frac{1}{5} =$

14. $1\frac{2}{7} + 6\frac{1}{6} =$

15. $3\frac{1}{4} + 4\frac{3}{5} =$

16. $6\frac{7}{8} + 1\frac{5}{6} =$

17. $7\frac{1}{2} + 2\frac{3}{7} =$

18. $3\frac{1}{10} + 1\frac{5}{8} =$

19. Rhonda needs 4 gallons of green paint to decorate her room. If she mixes $2\frac{1}{3}$ gallons of blue paint with $1\frac{1}{2}$ gallons of yellow paint, will she have enough? Explain.

_____

20. Ramona bought $1\frac{2}{3}$ pounds of strawberries, $2\frac{1}{4}$ pounds of apples and $2\frac{1}{2}$ pounds of oranges at the store. What was the total weight of Ramona's purchase? _____

Test Prep Circle the correct letter for the answer.

21. Find $1\frac{2}{5} + 5\frac{1}{6}$.

    A $6\frac{3}{11}$ **B** $5\frac{17}{30}$ **C** $6\frac{17}{30}$ **D** $6\frac{3}{30}$

22. It takes $2\frac{3}{4}$ hours to get to Cal City and $3\frac{5}{8}$ hours to get from Cal City to San Angelo. How long will it take to go to Cal City, then San Angelo?

    A $5\frac{3}{8}$ hours **B** 6 hours **C** 7 hours **D** $6\frac{3}{8}$ hours

Intervention Lesson **H35**

Subtracting Mixed Numbers

Example

Find $4\frac{1}{8} - 1\frac{2}{3}$.

Step 1 Write equivalent fractions with the LCD.

$4\frac{1}{8} = 4\frac{3}{24}$
$1\frac{2}{3} = 1\frac{16}{24}$

Step 2 Since $\frac{3}{24} < \frac{16}{24}$, rename $4\frac{3}{24}$ to show more twenty-fourths.

$4\frac{3}{24} = 3\frac{27}{24}$
$-1\frac{16}{24}$

Step 3 Subtract the fractions and the whole numbers. Simplify, if possible.

$3\frac{27}{24}$
$-1\frac{16}{24}$
$2\frac{11}{24}$

Estimate to check.
$4 - 2 = 2$

Subtract. Simplify, if possible. Estimate to check.

1. $2\frac{2}{3}$
   $-1\frac{1}{6}$

2. $2\frac{4}{10}$
   $-1\frac{3}{5}$

3. $5\frac{1}{4}$
   $-\frac{2}{5}$

4. $6\frac{7}{8}$
   $-1\frac{5}{6}$

5. $6\frac{3}{8}$
   $-5\frac{3}{4}$

6. 6
   $-3\frac{2}{9}$

7. $4\frac{1}{6}$
   $-2\frac{1}{4}$

8. $6\frac{1}{8}$
   $-4\frac{2}{16}$

69

Subtracting Mixed Numbers (continued)

Subtract. Simplify, if possible.

9. $2\frac{9}{10}$
    $-1\frac{5}{10}$

10. 5
    $-4\frac{2}{4}$

11. $\frac{2}{9}$
    $-\frac{2}{9}$

12. $4\frac{1}{5}$
    $-\frac{3}{5}$

13. $2\frac{3}{4} - 1 =$

14. $7\frac{2}{6} - 6\frac{5}{6} =$

15. $3\frac{2}{5} - 1\frac{2}{5} =$

16. $6\frac{1}{8} - 1\frac{5}{8} =$

17. $7 - 2\frac{3}{7} =$

18. $3\frac{4}{8} - 1\frac{7}{8} =$

19. $2\frac{1}{5} - 1\frac{1}{3} =$

20. $5\frac{1}{6} - 2\frac{1}{7} =$

21. $7\frac{5}{9} - 3\frac{2}{3} =$

22. **Mental Math** If you have $7\frac{3}{16}$ and you subtract $\frac{3}{16}$, how much do you have? _____

23. To make a dress, $1\frac{1}{6}$ yards of blue material is needed and $\frac{3}{4}$ yard of red material is needed. How much more blue material is needed than red material? _____

Test Prep Circle the correct letter for the answer.

24. Find $4\frac{2}{6} - 1\frac{5}{8}$.

   A $3\frac{17}{24}$ B $2\frac{17}{24}$ C $2\frac{3}{8}$ D $3\frac{3}{2}$

Name _____

Intervention Lesson **H36**

Math Diagnosis and Intervention System

Choose a Computation Method

Example 1

Find $8\frac{2}{7} + 4\frac{3}{7}$. Tell what computation method you used.

Step 1: Mentally add the whole numbers. $8 + 4 = 12$.

Step 2: Because the denominators are the same, mentally add the fractions. $\frac{2}{7} + \frac{3}{7} = \frac{5}{7}$.

Step 3: Write the sum, $12\frac{5}{7}$, and state that mental math was used.

Example 2

Find $9\frac{3}{8} - 4\frac{3}{4}$. Tell what computation method you used.

Step 1: Because the denominators are different, use paper and pencil to change the fractions to common denominators.

Step 2: Convert the $9\frac{3}{8}$ to the improper fraction $8\frac{11}{8}$.

Step 3: Subtract and state the computation method used.

$$\begin{array}{rl} 9\frac{3}{8} = & 8\frac{11}{8} \\ -4\frac{3}{4} = & -4\frac{6}{8} \\ \hline & 4\frac{5}{8} \end{array}$$; pencil and paper

---

Find the sum or difference. Tell what computation method you used.

1. $2\frac{5}{6} + 3\frac{1}{8} =$

2. $5\frac{4}{5} - 2\frac{1}{5} =$

_____ _____

3. $4\frac{9}{16} - 3\frac{7}{12} =$

4. $9\frac{2}{5} + 4\frac{3}{5} =$

_____ _____

71

Math Diagnosis and Intervention System

Name _____

Intervention Lesson **H36**

Choose a Computation Method (continued)

Find the sum or difference. Tell what computation method you used. All answers should be in simplest form.

5. $3\frac{2}{3} - 2\frac{1}{4} =$ _____

6. $9 - 2\frac{3}{8} =$ _____

7. $5\frac{8}{9} + 2\frac{2}{13} =$ _____

8. $6\frac{1}{8} + 5\frac{5}{24} =$ _____

Use the table for Questions 9–10.

Models	Length
Car	$7\frac{3}{8}$ in.
Boat	$8\frac{5}{12}$ in.
Airplane	$12\frac{9}{16}$ in.

9. How much longer is the model airplane than the car? _____

10. What is the total length of all three models? _____

11. Writing in Math Write a problem that would allow you to use mental math.

_____

Test Prep Circle the correct letter for the answer.

12. Find $6\frac{1}{8} + 5\frac{3}{4}$.

   A $11\frac{7}{8}$ **B** $11\frac{1}{3}$ **C** $\frac{3}{8}$ **D** $1\frac{5}{8}$

13. Find $17\frac{5}{8} - 3\frac{4}{15}$.

   A $20\frac{43}{120}$ **B** $20\frac{107}{120}$ **C** $14\frac{43}{120}$ **D** $14\frac{1}{7}$

Intervention Lesson **H37**

Multiplying Fractions by Whole Numbers

Example 1

Find $\frac{1}{6} \times 24$. Use mental math.

Step 1: Finding $\frac{1}{6}$ of 24 is the same as dividing 24 by 6.

Step 2: The result of dividing 24 by 6 is 4.

Step 3: So, $\frac{1}{6}$ of 24 is 4.

Example 2

Find $\frac{5}{6} \times 24$. Use mental math.

Step 1: Think: $\frac{5}{6}$ is five times $\frac{1}{6}$.

Step 2: $\frac{1}{6}$ of 24 is 4.

Step 3: Multiply: $4 \times 5 = 20$

Step 4: So $\frac{5}{6}$ of 24 is 20.

Find each product.

1. $\frac{8}{9} \times 45$

2. $42 \times \frac{3}{7}$

3. $\frac{7}{12}$ of 96

4. $\frac{2}{11} \times 77$

5. $\frac{3}{8} \times 64$

6. $\frac{1}{6}$ of 102

7. $\frac{2}{9} \times 72$

8. $\frac{3}{4} \times 168$

Name _____

Math Diagnosis and Intervention System
Intervention Lesson **H37**

Multiplying Fractions by Whole Numbers (continued)

Find each product.

9. $\frac{2}{5}$ of 25

10. $\frac{7}{9} \times 81$

11. $\frac{1}{2} \times 52$

12. $\frac{2}{3}$ of 66

13. four-sevenths of twenty-eight

14. three-fifths of forty-five

Use the information in the table for Questions 15–16.

Zoo Animals	Population	Zoo Animals	Population
Wild Dogs	10	Elephants	3
Monkeys	21	Tigers	8
Bears	18	Giraffes	5

15. If $\frac{2}{7}$ of the monkey population are spider monkeys, how many spider monkeys are at the zoo?

16. If $\frac{3}{5}$ of the animals listed are female, how many females are in the list?

17. You earned $141 babysitting last month. You promised your parents that you will save $\frac{2}{3}$ of your earnings. How much did you save last month?

18. Emperor penguins are approximately 45 inches tall, while rockhopper penguins are about $\frac{5}{9}$ of that height. How tall is a typical rockhopper penguin?

19. **Number Sense** If you know that $\frac{3}{4}$ of a number is 18, what is $\frac{1}{4}$ of the same number?

Test Prep Circle the correct letter for the answer.

20. What is $\frac{4}{9} \times 63$?

    A 7   B 28   C 36   D 142

21. What is five-sixths of forty-two?

    A 50   B 35   C 7   D $\frac{42}{56}$

Name _____

Intervention Lesson **H38**

Math Diagnosis and Intervention System

Estimating Products

Example 1

Estimate $3\frac{3}{4} \times 2\frac{1}{9}$.

Step 1 Round each mixed number to the nearest whole number.

$3\frac{3}{4} \longrightarrow 4$

$2\frac{1}{9} \longrightarrow 2$

Step 2 Multiply the whole numbers.

$4 \times 2 = 8$

Example 2

Estimate $\frac{1}{5} \times 41$.

Step 1 Change the whole number to the nearest number compatible with the denominator of the fraction.

$\frac{1}{5} \times 40$

Step 2 Simplify, then multiply.

$\frac{1}{\cancel{5}} \times \cancel{40}^{8} = 8$

Estimate.

1. $2\frac{7}{8} \times 7\frac{3}{5}$

2. $6\frac{1}{5} \times 8\frac{3}{4}$

3. $\frac{1}{2} \times 83$

_____   _____   _____

4. $5\frac{2}{7} \times 9\frac{4}{5}$

5. $\frac{1}{8} \times 75$

6. $\frac{2}{3} \times 26$

_____   _____   _____

7. $\frac{3}{4} \times 15$

8. $1\frac{5}{9} \times 7\frac{1}{2}$

9. $1\frac{1}{3} \times 5\frac{2}{9}$

_____   _____   _____

10. $4\frac{3}{12} \times 7$

11. $\frac{7}{9} \times 25$

12. $3\frac{11}{12} \times 9\frac{1}{10}$

_____   _____   _____

75

Estimating Products (continued)

Estimate.

13. $\frac{2}{5} \times 34$

14. $3\frac{5}{6} \times 1\frac{1}{8}$

15. $41 \times \frac{7}{8}$

16. $5\frac{7}{12} \times 1\frac{1}{5}$

17. $8\frac{5}{7} \times 1\frac{1}{3}$

18. $57 \times \frac{2}{7}$

19. $3\frac{5}{12} \times 1\frac{3}{5}$

20. $1\frac{9}{10} \times 6\frac{5}{7}$

21. $3\frac{4}{5} \times 5$

22. $\frac{2}{9} \times 59$

23. $2\frac{1}{5} \times 2\frac{1}{6}$

24. $73 \times \frac{4}{10}$

25. $\frac{2}{3} \times 10$

26. $\frac{1}{5} \times 23$

27. $\frac{2}{8} \times 65$

28. **Mental Math** Estimate $\frac{1}{2}$ of 81.

29. Mrs. Crabtree is having a dinner with 14 guests, including herself. She plans to buy $\frac{1}{4}$ pound of meat, 1 potato, and $\frac{1}{8}$ of a pie for each guest. Estimate how much meat she should buy.

Test Prep Circle the correct letter for the answer.

30. Estimate $2\frac{3}{4} \times 5\frac{8}{9}$.

    A 12   B 18   C 10   D 11

31. In her flower garden, Mrs. Taylor has 28 rose bushes. About $\frac{2}{3}$ of them are red. Estimate the number that are red.

    A 20   B 18   C 16   D 42

Name _____

Intervention Lesson **H39**

Math Diagnosis and Intervention System

Multiplying by a Fraction

Example

Find $\frac{3}{4} \times \frac{1}{9}$.

Step 1 Multiply the numerators.
$\frac{3}{4} \times \frac{1}{9} = \frac{3}{}$

Step 2 Multiply the denominators.
$\frac{3}{4} \times \frac{1}{9} = \frac{3}{36}$

Step 3 Simplify, if possible. $\frac{3}{36} = \frac{1}{12}$

Multiply. Simplify, if possible.

1. $\frac{1}{8} \times \frac{2}{3} =$ _____

2. $\frac{5}{6} \times \frac{1}{2} =$ _____

3. $\frac{1}{4} \times \frac{3}{5} =$ _____

4. $\frac{6}{7} \times \frac{1}{3} =$ _____

5. $\frac{3}{4} \times \frac{3}{8} =$ _____

6. $\frac{1}{5} \times \frac{4}{5} =$ _____

7. $\frac{2}{3} \times \frac{4}{7} =$ _____

8. $\frac{3}{7} \times \frac{3}{10} =$ _____

9. $\frac{4}{9} \times \frac{3}{4} =$ _____

10. $\frac{5}{8} \times \frac{4}{5} =$ _____

11. $\frac{7}{9} \times \frac{3}{5} =$ _____

12. $\frac{1}{10} \times \frac{5}{7} =$ _____

13. $\frac{7}{8} \times \frac{5}{14} =$ _____

14. $\frac{3}{11} \times \frac{1}{9} =$ _____

15. $\frac{1}{12} \times \frac{4}{5} =$ _____

77

Intervention Lesson **H39**

Name _____

Multiplying by a Fraction (continued)

Multiply. Simplify, if possible.

16. $\dfrac{2}{5} \times \dfrac{5}{7} =$ _____

17. $\dfrac{1}{3} \times \dfrac{3}{8} =$ _____

18. $\dfrac{1}{4} \times \dfrac{1}{4} =$ _____

19. $\dfrac{5}{12} \times \dfrac{3}{5} =$ _____

20. $\dfrac{9}{10} \times \dfrac{5}{7} =$ _____

21. $\dfrac{4}{5} \times \dfrac{5}{9} =$ _____

22. $\dfrac{2}{9} \times \dfrac{1}{6} =$ _____

23. $\dfrac{1}{5} \times \dfrac{1}{6} =$ _____

24. $\dfrac{5}{7} \times \dfrac{4}{10} =$ _____

25. Find $\dfrac{2}{3}$ of 9. _____

26. Find $\dfrac{1}{5}$ of 20. _____

27. Find $\dfrac{3}{8}$ of 10. _____

28. Find $\dfrac{3}{8}$ of 30. _____

29. Find $\dfrac{1}{10}$ of 20. _____

30. Find $\dfrac{3}{7}$ of 10. _____

Find the reciprocal of each number.

31. $\dfrac{3}{4}$ _____

32. $\dfrac{1}{15}$ _____

33. $\dfrac{7}{9}$ _____

34. $1\dfrac{3}{7}$ _____

35. **Mental Math** Find $\dfrac{1}{2}$ of 7. _____

36. There are 45 tents at the summer camp. Girls will use $\dfrac{2}{3}$ of the tents. How many tents will the girls use? _____

Test Prep Circle the correct letter for the answer.

37. Find $\dfrac{3}{4} \times \dfrac{8}{9}$.

   A $\dfrac{11}{36}$ **B** $\dfrac{24}{13}$ **C** $\dfrac{2}{3}$ **D** $\dfrac{3}{4}$

38. In her flower garden, Mrs. Taylor has 24 rose bushes. $\dfrac{5}{8}$ of them are red. How many rose bushes are red?

   A 36   **B** 15   **C** 8   **D** 6

Name _____

Intervention Lesson **H40**

Multiplying Fractions and Mixed Numbers

Example

Find $1\frac{3}{4} \times 2\frac{1}{9}$.

Step 1 Write the numbers as improper fractions.

$\frac{7}{4} \times \frac{19}{9}$

Step 2 Multiply the numerators and denominators.

$\frac{7}{4} \times \frac{19}{9} = \frac{133}{36}$

Step 3 Simplify, if possible.

$\frac{133}{36} = 3\frac{25}{36}$

Multiply. Simplify, if possible.

1. $\frac{1}{8} \times \frac{2}{3} =$ _____

2. $\frac{5}{6} \times \frac{1}{2} =$ _____

3. $\frac{1}{4} \times \frac{3}{5} =$ _____

4. $2\frac{6}{7} \times 1\frac{3}{4} =$ _____

5. $\frac{3}{4} \times 3\frac{1}{5} =$ _____

6. $1 \times 2\frac{4}{5} =$ _____

7. $\frac{2}{3} \times \frac{4}{7} =$ _____

8. $\frac{3}{7} \times \frac{3}{10} =$ _____

9. $\frac{4}{9} \times \frac{3}{4} =$ _____

10. $5\frac{5}{8} \times 3\frac{4}{5} =$

11. $2\frac{2}{7} \times 5\frac{3}{5} =$

12. $2\frac{1}{10} \times 2\frac{1}{7} =$

_____

_____

_____

13. $12 + \left(\frac{7}{8} \times 5\frac{5}{14}\right) =$

14. $3 + \left(1\frac{1}{4} \times 1\frac{1}{9}\right) =$

15. $4\frac{1}{12} \times \frac{4}{5} =$

_____

_____

_____

Name _____

Intervention Lesson **H40**

Multiplying Fractions and Mixed Numbers (continued)

Multiply. Simplify, if possible.

16. $\dfrac{2}{5} \times \dfrac{5}{7} =$ _____

17. $\dfrac{1}{3} \times \dfrac{3}{8} =$ _____

18. $\dfrac{1}{4} \times \dfrac{1}{4} =$ _____

19. $13 + \left(\dfrac{5}{12} \times 1\dfrac{3}{5}\right) =$ _____

20. $2\dfrac{1}{10} \times 6\dfrac{5}{7} =$ _____

21. $3\dfrac{4}{5} \times 5 =$ _____

22. $\dfrac{2}{9} \times \dfrac{1}{6} =$ _____

23. $\dfrac{1}{5} \times \dfrac{1}{6} =$ _____

24. $\dfrac{5}{7} \times \dfrac{4}{10} =$ _____

25. **Math Reasoning** If you forget to simplify before multiplying, will you still get the same answer if you simplify after multiplying? _____

26. Pam is making a cake. The recipe calls for $2\dfrac{1}{8}$ cups of flour. How much flour is needed for 4 cakes? _____

27. Marsha has 10 red beads that are $1\dfrac{2}{5}$ inches long and 4 blue beads that are $1\dfrac{1}{16}$ inches long. How long will her necklace be if she uses all the beads? _____

Test Prep Circle the correct letter for the answer.

28. Find $2\dfrac{3}{4} \times 3\dfrac{1}{9}$.

   A $8\dfrac{5}{9}$ B $6\dfrac{3}{36}$ C $6\dfrac{1}{12}$ D $\dfrac{99}{28}$

29. Lois walks $1\dfrac{4}{5}$ miles every day. How far does she walk in a week?

   A $7\dfrac{28}{35}$ B $12\dfrac{3}{5}$ C 14   D $11\dfrac{3}{5}$

Understanding Division with Fractions

In this lesson, you will divide a whole number by a fraction using an inch-ruler.

Example 1

Measure the line above in inches. It is _____ inches long.

Suppose you cut the line into pieces that are each $\frac{1}{2}$ inch long.

Guess how many pieces there would be. _____

Now, starting at the left, use your ruler to mark lengths of $\frac{1}{2}$ inch.

How many $\frac{1}{2}$-inch lengths did you get? _____

What you did was divide 5 by $\frac{1}{2}$.

$5 \div \frac{1}{2} = 10$

Example 2

Measure the line above. It is _____ inches long.

Here is a way to show that $6 \div \frac{3}{4} = 8$.

Starting at the left, mark the line into pieces, each $\frac{3}{4}$ inch long.

How many $\frac{3}{4}$-inch lengths are there? _____

So, if you divide 6 by $\frac{3}{4}$, you get 8.

You can also multiply by the reciprocal of the divisor.

$6 \div \frac{3}{4} = 6 \times \frac{4}{3} = \frac{6}{1} \times \frac{4}{3} = \frac{24}{3} = 8$

Find the number of lengths. Draw a line and use your ruler if you wish.

1. How many $\frac{1}{4}$s are in 2? _____

2. How many $\frac{1}{2}$s are in 3? _____

3. How many $\frac{1}{4}$s are in 4? _____

4. How many $\frac{3}{4}$s are in 3? _____

Name _____

Intervention Lesson **H41**

Understanding Division with Fractions (continued)

Find each quotient. Draw a line and use your ruler to help you if you wish.

5. How many $\frac{1}{8}$s are in 2? _____
6. How many $\frac{2}{8}$s are in 1? _____

7. How many $\frac{3}{8}$s are in 3? _____
8. How many $\frac{6}{8}$s are in 3? _____

Find each quotient.

9. $3 \div \frac{1}{6}$ _____
10. $9 \div \frac{3}{5}$ _____
11. $4 \div \frac{1}{4}$ _____

12. $10 \div \frac{5}{6}$ _____
13. $9 \div \frac{3}{4}$ _____
14. $6 \div \frac{1}{3}$ _____

15. $2 \div \frac{1}{7}$ _____
16. $6 \div \frac{3}{5}$ _____
17. $10 \div \frac{1}{10}$ _____

18. Number Sense Sometimes you get the same number if you divide a whole number by a fraction that you would if you multiply the whole number by the denominator of the fraction. Give an example of such a fraction. [Hint: Look at problems 9, 11, 15, and 17, above.]

_____

Test Prep Circle the correct letter for the answer.

19. $12 \div \frac{2}{3}$

A 8   **B** 18   **C** 6   **D** 36

20. $15 \div \frac{3}{5}$

A 45   **B** 9   **C** 25   **D** 75

Name _____

Intervention Lesson **H42**

Math Diagnosis and Intervention System

Dividing Fractions

Example

Find $\frac{3}{4} \div \frac{1}{9}$.

Step 1 Multiply by the reciprocal of the divisor.

$\frac{3}{4} \times \frac{9}{1}$

Step 2 Multiply the numerators and denominators.

$\frac{3}{4} \times \frac{9}{1} = \frac{27}{4}$

Step 3 Simplify, if possible. $\frac{27}{4} = 6\frac{3}{4}$

Divide. Simplify, if possible.

1. $\frac{1}{8} \div \frac{2}{3} =$ _____

2. $\frac{5}{6} \div \frac{1}{2} =$ _____

3. $\frac{1}{4} \div \frac{3}{5} =$ _____

4. $\frac{6}{7} \div \frac{3}{4} =$ _____

5. $\frac{3}{4} \div \frac{3}{8} =$ _____

6. $\frac{1}{5} \div \frac{4}{5} =$ _____

7. $\frac{2}{3} \div \frac{4}{7} =$ _____

8. $\frac{3}{7} \div \frac{3}{10} =$ _____

9. $\frac{4}{9} \div \frac{3}{4} =$ _____

10. $\frac{5}{8} \div \frac{4}{5} =$ _____

11. $\frac{7}{9} \div \frac{3}{5} =$ _____

12. $\frac{1}{10} \div \frac{5}{7} =$ _____

13. $\frac{7}{8} \div \frac{5}{14} =$ _____

14. $\frac{3}{11} \div \frac{1}{9} =$ _____

15. $\frac{1}{12} \div \frac{4}{5} =$ _____

Dividing Fractions (continued)

Divide. Simplify, if possible.

16. $\dfrac{2}{5} \div \dfrac{5}{7} = $ _____

17. $\dfrac{1}{3} \div \dfrac{3}{8} = $ _____

18. $\dfrac{1}{4} \div \dfrac{1}{4} = $ _____

19. $\dfrac{5}{12} \div \dfrac{3}{5} = $ _____

20. $\dfrac{9}{10} \div \dfrac{5}{7} = $ _____

21. $\dfrac{4}{5} \div \dfrac{5}{9} = $ _____

22. $\dfrac{2}{9} \div \dfrac{1}{6} = $ _____

23. $\dfrac{1}{5} \div \dfrac{1}{6} = $ _____

24. $\dfrac{5}{7} \div \dfrac{4}{10} = $ _____

25. **Mental Math** How many $\dfrac{1}{4}$'s are there in 10? _____

26. Bonnie is cutting 7 apples. Each apple is cut into eighths. How many slices of apple will she have? _____

27. In the school cafeteria, 15 pounds of vegetables were ordered. If each student usually gets $\dfrac{3}{8}$ of a pound of vegetables, how many students could be fed with those that were ordered? _____

Test Prep Circle the correct letter for the answer.

28. Find $\dfrac{3}{4} \div \dfrac{8}{9}$.

    A $\dfrac{32}{27}$ B $\dfrac{27}{32}$ C $\dfrac{2}{3}$ D $\dfrac{3}{2}$

29. How many $\dfrac{3}{5}$-foot bricks are needed to go across a 15 foot wall?

    A 25   B 20   C 9   D 15

Math Diagnosis and Intervention System

Intervention Lesson **H43**

Name _____

Multiplying and Dividing Mixed Numbers

Example

Find $1\frac{3}{4} \div 2\frac{1}{9}$.

Step 1 Write the numbers as improper fractions.

$\frac{7}{4} \div \frac{19}{9}$

Step 2 Multiply the reciprocal of the divisor.

$\frac{7}{4} \times \frac{9}{19}$

Step 3 Simplify, if possible. $\frac{63}{76}$

Multiply or divide. Simplify, if possible.

1. $1 \div 2\frac{2}{3} =$ _____

2. $5 \times \frac{1}{2} =$ _____

3. $3\frac{1}{4} \times 1\frac{3}{5} =$ _____

4. $2\frac{6}{7} \div 1\frac{3}{4} =$ _____

5. $\frac{3}{4} \times 3\frac{1}{5} =$ _____

6. $1 \div 2\frac{4}{5} =$ _____

7. $4\frac{2}{3} \times 1\frac{4}{7} =$ _____

8. $2\frac{1}{7} \times 2\frac{1}{10} =$ _____

9. $1\frac{4}{9} \div 4 =$ _____

10. $5\frac{5}{8} \times 3\frac{4}{5} =$ _____

11. $3\frac{7}{9} \div 5\frac{5}{3} =$ _____

12. $2\frac{1}{10} \times 2\frac{1}{7} =$ _____

13. $2\frac{7}{8} \div 5\frac{5}{14} =$ _____

14. $3 \times 1\frac{1}{9} =$ _____

15. $4\frac{1}{12} \times \frac{4}{5} =$ _____

85

Name _____

Intervention Lesson **H43**

Math Diagnosis and Intervention System

Multiplying and Dividing Mixed Numbers (continued)

Multiply or divide. Simplify, if possible.

16. $3\frac{2}{5} \times \frac{5}{7} =$ _____   **17.** $2\frac{1}{3} \times 1\frac{3}{8} =$ _____   **18.** $3\frac{1}{4} \div 4\frac{1}{4} =$ _____

19. $3\frac{5}{12} \div 1\frac{3}{5} =$ _____   **20.** $1\frac{9}{10} \times 2\frac{5}{7} =$ _____   **21.** $3\frac{4}{5} \div 5 =$ _____

22. $2\frac{2}{9} \times 5\frac{1}{16} =$ _____   **23.** $2\frac{1}{5} \times 1\frac{1}{6} =$ _____   **24.** $7 \div 3\frac{4}{10} =$ _____

25. Math Reasoning If you are dividing and the divisor is bigger than the dividend, then will the quotient be more or less than one? _____

26. Pam is making a necklace. She has large beads that are $1\frac{1}{8}$ inches long. How many beads are needed to make a necklace 18 inches long? _____

27. Marsha is making a giant sandwich. There will be 6 cheese sections that are $3\frac{1}{3}$ inches long and 5 vegetable sections that are $4\frac{3}{8}$ inches long. How long is the sandwich? _____

Test Prep Circle the correct letter for the answer.

28. Find $2\frac{3}{4} \times 3\frac{1}{9}$.

  A $8\frac{5}{9}$ **B** $6\frac{3}{36}$ **C** $6\frac{1}{12}$ **D** $\frac{99}{28}$

Name _____

Intervention Practice **H1**

Multiples, Factors, and Divisibility

Circle the correct letter for the answer.

1. Which number is divisible by 2, 3, and 10?
   - A 345
   - B 500
   - C 605
   - D 1,290

2. Which number is divisible by 2, 3, 6 and 9?
   - A 21
   - B 84
   - C 198
   - D 436

3. Which set of numbers is 255 divisible by?
   - A 2, 3, 4, 6, 9
   - B 2, 3, 6, 9
   - C 3, 4, 9
   - D 3, 5

4. Which number is divisible by 9?
   - A 3824
   - B 3834
   - C 3854
   - D 3874

5. Jason has 156 campers that he needs to divide into even groups. Which set of groups could he divide the campers into?
   - A 2
   - B 2, 3
   - C 2, 3, 4, 6
   - D 2, 3, 4, 5, 6, 9

6. Which number is a multiple of 10?
   - A 210
   - B 302
   - C 4006
   - D 7041

7. Which number is divisible by 2, 3, 4 and 9?
   - A 479
   - B 843
   - C 3,459
   - D 6,156

8. What set of numbers is 8,214 divisible by?
   - A 2, 5
   - B 2, 3, 6
   - C 2, 3, 4, 6
   - D 2, 3, 4, 6, 9

87

Name _____

Math Diagnosis and Intervention System

Intervention Practice **H2**

Factoring Numbers

Circle the correct letter for the answer.

1. Which of the following is divisible by 6?
   - **A** 11
   - **B** 2
   - **C** 42
   - **D** 73

2. Which are all the factors of 50?
   - **A** 1, 2, 5, 10, 25, 50
   - **B** 1, 2, 5, 10, 50
   - **C** 1, 2, 4, 5, 10, 25, 50
   - **D** 1, 2, 5, 10, 15, 25, 100

3. Which of the following is a factor pair of 72?
   - **A** 12 and 5
   - **B** 7 and 9
   - **C** 9 and 9
   - **D** 9 and 8

4. Which number is divisible by 3?
   - **A** 46
   - **B** 58
   - **C** 96
   - **D** 101

5. Which number is not divisible by 3?
   - **A** 51
   - **B** 47
   - **C** 39
   - **D** 24

6. There are 60 seats to be set up in the auditorium. There must be an equal number of seats in each row. Which pattern is NOT correct?
   - **A** 6 rows, 10 seats in each
   - **B** 5 rows, 12 seats in each
   - **C** 4 rows, 16 seats in each
   - **D** 3 rows, 20 seats in each

7. Which are all the factors of 45?
   - **A** 1, 5, 9, 45
   - **B** 1, 3, 6, 9, 12, 45
   - **C** 1, 3, 5, 9, 15, 45
   - **D** 1, 5, 7, 9, 45

8. Which are all the factors of 35?
   - **A** 1, 5, 7, 35
   - **B** 1, 3, 11, 35
   - **C** 1, 5, 9, 35
   - **D** 5, 7, 35

Name _____

Intervention Practice **H3**

Prime Factorization

Circle the correct letter for the answer.

1. Which statement is true about a prime number?

    A It has exactly three factors.
    B It must be an odd number.
    C It must be greater than 10.
    D It has exactly 2 factors, itself and 1.

2. Which is the prime factorization of 48?

    A $2^3 \times 3$ **C** 3×16
    B $2^4 \times 3$ **D** 6×8

3. Which number is composite?

    A 24   **C** 53
    B 31   **D** 97

4. Which is the prime factorization of 180?

    A $2 \times 3^2 \times 10$
    B 5×3^4
    C $2^2 \times 3^2 \times 5$
    D $2 \times 5 \times 18$

5. Which is *not* a prime number?

    A 51   **C** 43
    B 47   **D** 41

6. Which is a prime number?

    A 1   **C** 27
    B 17   **D** 39

7. What is the prime factorization of 495?

    A $5 \times 11 \times 3^2$ **C** 5×11^2
    B $5 \times 11 \times 3$ **D** $5 \times 11 \times 9$

8. Which number is not composite?

    A 35   **C** 57
    B 49   **D** 61

9. Which expression shows 100 as a product of prime factors?

    A 4×25 **C** $2^2 \times 5^2$
    B 10×10 **D** $2^3 \times 5^2$

10. Ciandra lives on a block with house numbers from 31 to 61. If everyone on the block has a prime house number, how many houses are there on the block?

    A 2 houses   **C** 8 houses
    B 6 houses   **D** 15 houses

Name _____

Intervention Practice **H4**

Math Diagnosis and Intervention System

Greatest Common Factor

Circle the correct letter for the answer.

1. Which list shows all the common factors of 24 and 30?

   A 1, 2, 3
   B 1, 2, 3, 4, 5, 6, 8, 10, 12, 15, 24, 30
   C 1, 2, 3, 6
   D 1, 2, 3, 6, 12

2. What is the GCF of 45 and 90?

   A 5
   B 10
   C 15
   D 45

3. The Art teacher has 36 small sticks and 60 pipe cleaners for art projects. He wants to make up kits for the students using all the sticks and pipe cleaners. All the kits must be alike. He wants to make as many kits as possible. What is the greatest number of kits he can make?

   A 8 kits
   B 9 kits
   C 12 kits
   D 36 kits

4. What is the GCF of 15 and 20?

   A 3
   B 4
   C 5
   D 9

5. What is the GCF of 16 and 20?

   A 8
   B 4
   C 2
   D 1

6. Louise is making bags of party favors. She has 16 stickers and 24 candies. She wants each bag to be alike, and she needs to use all of the stickers and candies. What is the greatest number of party bags she can make?

   A 2 bags   **C** 8 bags
   B 4 bags   **D** 16 bags

7. Heather picked 20 roses and 30 carnations. She wants to make identical bouquets that have the same combination of roses and carnations, but the combination doesn't have to have an equal number of roses and carnations. What is the greatest number of bouquets she can make?

   A 5 bouquets
   B 10 bouquets
   C 15 bouquets
   D 30 bouquets

8. What is the GCF of 12 and 18?

   A 2   **C** 6
   B 3   **D** 9

Name _____

Intervention Practice **H5**

Math Diagnosis and Intervention System

Least Common Multiple

Circle the correct letter for the answer.

1. Find the LCM for 6 and 14.
   - A 2
   - B 42
   - C 48
   - D 84

2. Ken goes to the orthodontist every 3 weeks. Linda goes to the orthodontist every 4 weeks. Paul goes to the orthodontist every 5 weeks. Today, they were all at the orthodontist together. In how many weeks will they all be together at the orthodontist again?
   - A 15 weeks
   - B 30 weeks
   - C 45 weeks
   - D 60 weeks

3. Judy buys balloons in packages of 6. She buys colored string for the balloons in packages of 4. What is the smallest number of packages of string she should purchase to be sure she has the same number of balloons and strings?
   - A 12
   - B 24
   - C 3
   - D 20

4. Find the LCM for 10 and 15.
   - A 20
   - B 30
   - C 40
   - D 60

5. Find the LCM for 6, 8, and 12.
   - A 12
   - B 18
   - C 24
   - D 48

6. The airport bus arrives at the bus station every 32 minutes. The city bus arrives at the bus station every 6 minutes. To find out how often both buses arrive at the bus station at the same time, find the least common multiple of 32 and 6.
   - A Every 36 minutes
   - B Every 64 minutes
   - C Every 96 minutes
   - D Every 128 minutes

7. What is the LCM of 9 and 12?
   - A 12
   - B 18
   - C 36
   - D 72

8. Sheila records the outdoor temperature every 3 hours. She records the wind rate every 5 hours. If she just recorded both the temperature and the wind rate, in how many hours will she again record both the temperature and the wind rate?
   - A 5 hours
   - B 10 hours
   - C 15 hours
   - D 30 hours

Name _____

Intervention Practice **H6**

Equal Parts of a Whole

Circle the correct letter for the answer.

Use the figures to answer Questions 1–3.

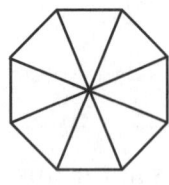

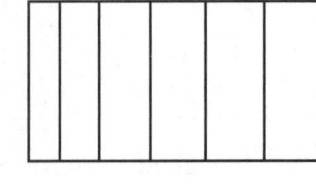

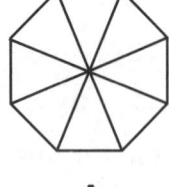

A   B   C   D

1. In what way is figure C divided?
   A unequal parts   C fourths
   B fifths   D halves

2. Which figure is not divided into equal parts?
   A figure A   C figure B
   B figure C   D figure D

3. Which figure is divided into eighths?
   A figure A   C figure B
   B figure C   D figure D

4. Name the equal parts when a submarine sandwich is cut into equal parts for 6 people.
   A thirds   C tenths
   B sixths   D fourths

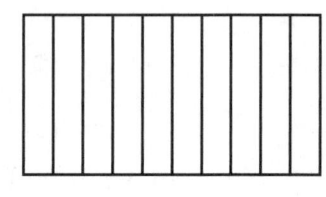

5. A yardstick is 36 inches. If it is divided into 3 equal parts, how long is each part?
   A 18 inches   C 3 inches
   B 6 inches   D 12 inches

6. How many equal parts are there when a whole is divided into fourths?
   A 3   C 5
   B 4   D 6

7. If you share a whole pie equally with four friends, how many equal pieces will you have?
   A 6   C 5
   B 3   D 4

8. How many equal parts are there when a rectangle is divided into fifths?
   A 2   C 4
   B 10   D 5

Name _____

Intervention Practice **H7**

Naming Fractional Parts

Circle the correct letter for the answer.

Use the figures to answer Questions 1–4.

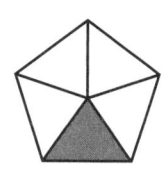

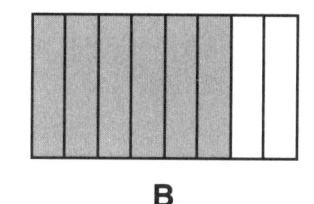

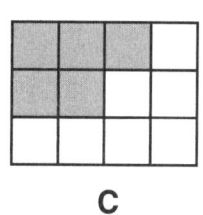

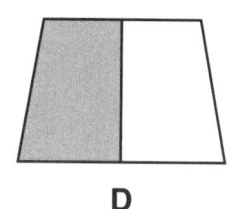

A   B   C   D

1. Which figure shows the fraction $\frac{5}{12}$?
   A figure A   C figure B
   B figure C   D figure D

2. Which figure shows two equal halves?
   A figure A   C figure B
   B figure C   D figure D

3. What fraction of figure B is shaded?
   A $\frac{6}{8}$ C $\frac{5}{8}$
   B $\frac{8}{12}$ D $\frac{1}{5}$

4. What fraction of figure A is shaded?
   A $\frac{4}{5}$ C $\frac{1}{5}$
   B $\frac{1}{4}$ D $\frac{1}{2}$

5. What is the name for the number in a fraction that tells how many equal parts in all?
   A fraction   C numerator
   B denominator   D figure

6. What is the name for the number in a fraction that tells how many equal parts are shaded?
   A fraction   C numerator
   B denominator   D figure

7. A flag has 6 stripes of equal size. Two of the stripes are red. What fraction of the flag is red?
   A $\frac{1}{6}$ C $\frac{4}{6}$
   B $\frac{2}{6}$ D $\frac{2}{3}$

8. A flag has 6 stripes of equal size. Three of the stripes are blue. What fraction of the flag is blue?
   A $\frac{2}{3}$ C $\frac{1}{6}$
   B $\frac{2}{6}$ D $\frac{3}{6}$

Name _____

Intervention Practice **H8**

Finding Equivalent Fractions

Circle the correct letter for the answer.

1. Use the fraction models. Which number belongs in the ■?

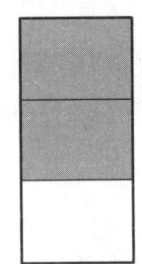

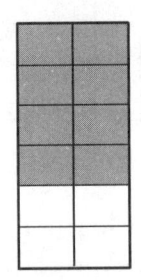

   $\frac{2}{3} = \frac{\blacksquare}{12}$

   A 2   C 6
   B 4   D 8

2. Use the fraction models. Which number belongs in the ■?

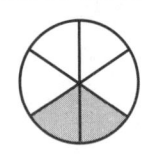

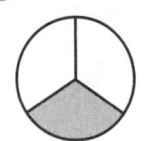

   $\frac{2}{6} = \frac{\blacksquare}{3}$

   A 1   C 3
   B 2   D 4

3. Which fraction is equivalent to $\frac{1}{4}$?

   A $\frac{2}{5}$ C $\frac{3}{12}$
   B $\frac{4}{1}$ D $\frac{4}{8}$

4. Use the fraction models. Which number belongs in the ■?

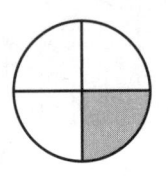

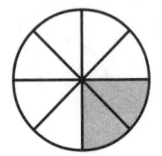

   $\frac{1}{4} = \frac{\blacksquare}{8}$

   A 1   C 3
   B 2   D 6

5. Lou ate $\frac{3}{5}$ of his sandwich. Martha ate the same amount of her sandwich. How many tenths did Martha eat?

   A $\frac{2}{10}$ C $\frac{6}{10}$
   B $\frac{4}{10}$ D $\frac{8}{10}$

6. Use the fraction models. Which number belongs in the ■?

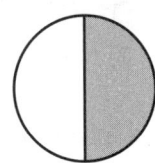

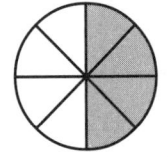

   $\frac{1}{2} = \frac{\blacksquare}{8}$

   A 1
   B 2
   C 3
   D 4

Name _____

Intervention Practice **H9**

Comparing and Ordering Fractions

Circle the correct letter for the answer.

1. Use the fraction models. Which is true?

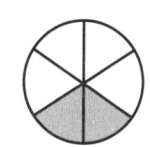

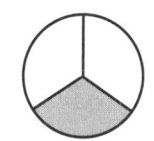

   A $\frac{2}{6} > \frac{1}{3}$ C $\frac{2}{6} < \frac{1}{3}$

   B $\frac{2}{6} = \frac{1}{3}$ D $\frac{1}{2} < \frac{1}{3}$

2. Which fraction is the least?

   A $\frac{5}{8}$ C $\frac{1}{8}$

   B $\frac{2}{3}$ D $\frac{1}{3}$

3. Which numbers are in order from greatest to least?

   A $\frac{1}{4}, \frac{1}{3}, \frac{3}{8}$

   B $\frac{1}{3}, \frac{3}{8}, \frac{1}{4}$

   C $\frac{3}{8}, \frac{1}{3}, \frac{1}{4}$

   D $\frac{3}{8}, \frac{1}{4}, \frac{1}{3}$

4. Which of the these number sentences is correct?

   A $\frac{2}{3} > \frac{4}{6}$ C $\frac{1}{4} = \frac{2}{3}$

   B $\frac{1}{2} < \frac{3}{10}$ D $\frac{4}{6} > \frac{1}{3}$

5. Which fraction is the greatest?

   A $\frac{1}{4}$ C $\frac{1}{2}$

   B $\frac{5}{8}$ D $\frac{3}{4}$

6. Use the fraction models. Which is true?

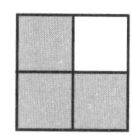

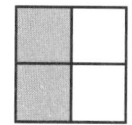

   A $\frac{3}{4} < \frac{2}{4}$ C $\frac{3}{4} > \frac{2}{4}$

   B $\frac{3}{4} = \frac{2}{4}$ D $\frac{1}{4} > \frac{2}{4}$

7. Mrs. Marshall sold pieces of cake at the school fair. The table below shows the fraction of each cake that was sold.

Cake Flavor	Amount Sold
Chocolate	$\frac{1}{2}$
Vanilla	$\frac{1}{3}$
Banana	$\frac{1}{8}$
Orange	$\frac{1}{4}$

   Of which cake was the least amount sold?

   A Chocolate   C Banana
   B Vanilla   D Orange

Intervention Practice **H10**

Estimating Fractional Amounts

Fill in the ○ for the correct answer.

How much is left? Estimate.

1. 
- ○ about $\frac{1}{3}$
- ○ about $\frac{1}{2}$
- ○ about $\frac{1}{4}$
- ○ about $\frac{2}{4}$

2. 
- ○ about $\frac{1}{2}$
- ○ about $\frac{1}{4}$
- ○ about $\frac{3}{4}$
- ○ about $\frac{2}{3}$

3. 
- ○ about $\frac{1}{2}$
- ○ about $\frac{5}{6}$
- ○ about $\frac{3}{4}$
- ○ about $\frac{1}{3}$

4. 
- ○ about $\frac{1}{3}$
- ○ about $\frac{1}{4}$
- ○ about $\frac{1}{2}$
- ○ about $\frac{3}{4}$

5. 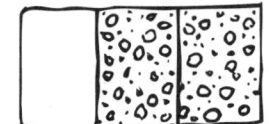
- ○ about $\frac{1}{2}$
- ○ about $\frac{5}{6}$
- ○ about $\frac{3}{4}$
- ○ about $\frac{2}{3}$

6. 
- ○ about $\frac{1}{3}$
- ○ about $\frac{1}{2}$
- ○ about $\frac{2}{3}$
- ○ about $\frac{3}{4}$

96

Intervention Practice **H11**

Fractions on the Number Line

Circle the correct letter for the answer.

1. Which fraction is the same as 1 whole?

   A $\frac{1}{2}$ C $\frac{2}{4}$

   B $\frac{3}{3}$ D $\frac{4}{3}$

2. Write the missing fractions for the number line.

   [number line: 0, 1/5, ▪, 3/5, ▪, 1]

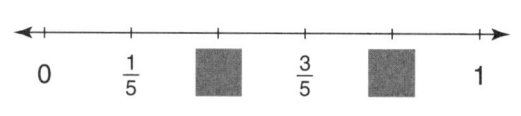

   A $\frac{2}{5}, \frac{5}{5}$ C $\frac{2}{5}, \frac{4}{5}$

   B $\frac{3}{5}, \frac{4}{5}$ D $\frac{1}{5}, \frac{2}{5}$

Use the number lines to answer Questions 3–5.

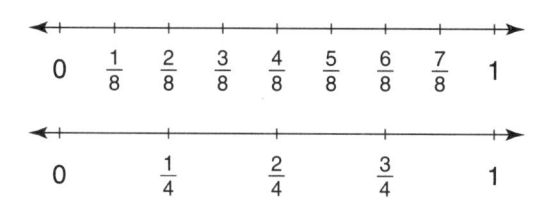

[number line: 0, 1/8, 2/8, 3/8, 4/8, 5/8, 6/8, 7/8, 1]

[number line: 0, 1/4, 2/4, 3/4, 1]

3. Which fraction on the second number line is equal to $\frac{4}{8}$?

   A $\frac{2}{3}$ C $\frac{1}{4}$

   B $\frac{3}{4}$ D $\frac{2}{4}$

4. Which fraction is greatest?

   A $\frac{2}{8}$ C $\frac{5}{8}$

   B $\frac{3}{4}$ D $\frac{2}{4}$

5. Which fraction on the first number line is greater than $\frac{3}{4}$?

   A $\frac{7}{8}$ C $\frac{4}{8}$

   B $\frac{3}{8}$ D $\frac{6}{8}$

6. Write the missing fractions for the number line.

   [number line: 0, ▪, 2/6, 3/6, ▪, 5/6, 1]

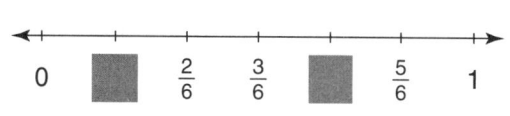

   A $\frac{1}{6}, \frac{5}{6}$ C $\frac{1}{6}, \frac{4}{6}$

   B $\frac{2}{6}, \frac{4}{6}$ D $\frac{1}{6}, \frac{3}{6}$

7. Which fraction is not the same as 1 whole?

   A $\frac{4}{4}$ C $\frac{2}{2}$

   B $\frac{5}{5}$ D $\frac{3}{4}$

Name _____

Intervention Practice **H12**

Parts of a Region

Circle the correct letter for the answer.

1. What fraction of the figure is not shaded?

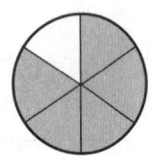

   A $\frac{1}{6}$ C $\frac{1}{3}$

   B $\frac{1}{4}$ D $\frac{5}{6}$

2. Which of these quilt pieces is exactly $\frac{3}{8}$ shaded?

   A 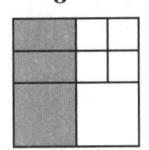   C

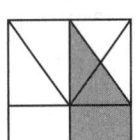

   B 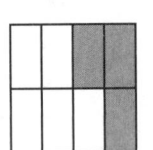   D

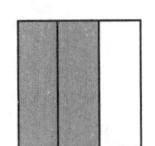

3. A flag is divided into 6 equal parts. Two of the parts are red. What fraction of the flag is not red?

   A $\frac{1}{6}$ C $\frac{3}{6}$

   B $\frac{2}{6}$ D $\frac{4}{6}$

4. Which of these tile designs is exactly $\frac{3}{4}$ white?

   A    C

   B 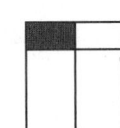   D

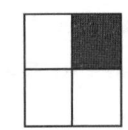

5. Marco spends 8 hours a day at school. He spends 2 hours a day in language arts and 1 hour in math. What fraction of his school day does he spend in language arts?

   A $\frac{1}{8}$ C $\frac{3}{8}$

   B $\frac{2}{8}$ D $\frac{1}{2}$

6. Antonio was washing the patio door. The door had 12 panes of glass. He washed 5 of them, then he went to eat lunch. What fraction of the panes had he washed?

   A $\frac{1}{12}$ C $\frac{7}{12}$

   B $\frac{5}{12}$ D $\frac{5}{7}$

98

Intervention Practice **H13**

Fractions and Sets

Circle the correct letter for the answer.

What fraction of the counters are shaded?

1.

A $\frac{4}{5}$ C $\frac{1}{5}$

B $\frac{5}{5}$ D $\frac{1}{4}$

2.

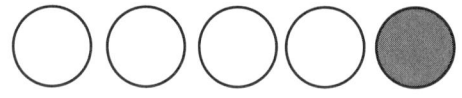

A $\frac{4}{6}$ C $\frac{2}{6}$

B $\frac{2}{5}$ D $\frac{1}{2}$

3. Which picture shows $\frac{2}{3}$ of the triangles shaded?

A   B   C   D

4. Find $\frac{1}{5}$ of 25.

A 4 C 6
B 5 D 10

Use the picture to answer Questions 5–7.

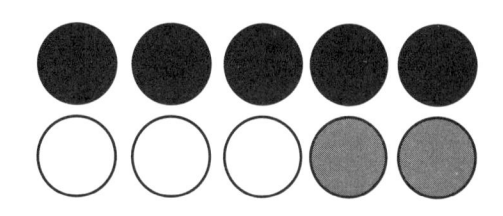

5. What fraction of the counters are gray?

A $\frac{2}{5}$ C $\frac{2}{10}$

B $\frac{3}{10}$ D $\frac{2}{8}$

6. What fraction of the counters are black?

A $\frac{5}{10}$ C $\frac{2}{10}$

B $\frac{3}{8}$ D $\frac{3}{10}$

7. What fraction of the counters are white?

A $\frac{3}{8}$ C $\frac{2}{10}$

B $\frac{3}{10}$ D $\frac{5}{10}$

Parts of a Set

Circle the correct letter for the answer.

1. Which group of circles has exactly $\frac{5}{8}$ white circles?

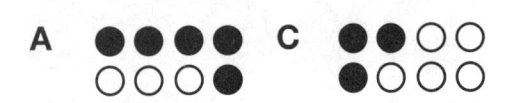

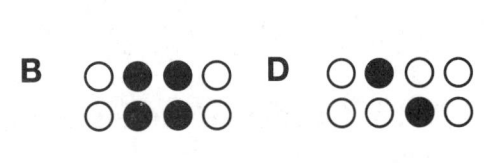

    A ●●●● / ○○○●
    B ○●●○ / ○●●○
    C ●●○○ / ●○○○
    D ○●○○ / ○○●○

2. What fraction of these dots is shaded?

    A $\frac{5}{12}$ C $\frac{12}{5}$
    B $\frac{5}{7}$ D $\frac{7}{12}$

3. Trevor has 9 marbles. Two of them are blue and 3 are green. The rest of the marbles are red. What fraction of the marbles is red?

    A $\frac{2}{9}$ C $\frac{4}{9}$
    B $\frac{3}{9}$ D $\frac{5}{9}$

4. Allen has 8 crayons in a box. He breaks 2 red crayons and 1 blue one. What fraction of the crayons is not broken?

    A $\frac{1}{8}$ C $\frac{3}{8}$
    B $\frac{2}{8}$ D $\frac{5}{8}$

5. Which fraction shows the part of the group that is shaded?

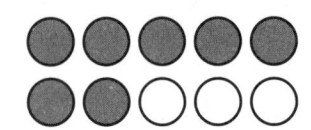

    A $\frac{7}{10}$ C $\frac{5}{10}$
    B $\frac{7}{1}$ D $\frac{3}{10}$

6. Candice has 3 red apples, 4 green apples, and 5 yellow apples. What fraction of the apples is green?

    A $\frac{8}{12}$ C $\frac{4}{12}$
    B $\frac{4}{8}$ D $\frac{3}{12}$

7. A bag has 10 oranges. You use 6 oranges to make juice. What fraction of the oranges do you use to make juice?

    A $\frac{4}{10}$ C $\frac{4}{6}$
    B $\frac{6}{10}$ D $\frac{6}{4}$

Intervention Practice **H15**

Mixed Numbers

Circle the correct letter for the answer.

1. The distance from Springfield to Middleton measures $1\frac{3}{4}$ inches on the map. Which is the distance written as an improper fraction?

   A $\frac{6}{4}$ C $\frac{9}{4}$

   B $\frac{7}{4}$ D $\frac{13}{4}$

2. How is the improper fraction $\frac{20}{8}$ written as a mixed number?

   A 2   C $3\frac{1}{2}$

   B $2\frac{4}{8}$ D $3\frac{5}{8}$

3. Which fraction describes the shaded areas?

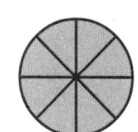

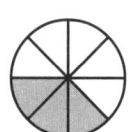

   A $\frac{3}{8}$ C $\frac{19}{8}$

   B $\frac{8}{19}$ D $\frac{24}{8}$

4. Which letter is at $2\frac{1}{4}$ on the number line?

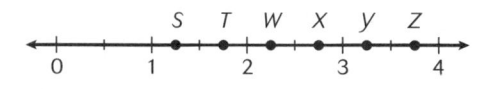

   A T   C V
   B U   D W

5. Which number does Point R represent?

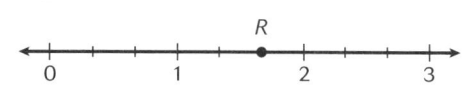

   A $\frac{3}{5}$ C $\frac{5}{3}$

   B $\frac{2}{3}$ D 5

6. How is the improper fraction $\frac{23}{6}$ written as a mixed number?

   A $4\frac{1}{6}$ C $3\frac{2}{3}$

   B $3\frac{5}{6}$ D 3

7. Melissa's puppy weighs $8\frac{1}{8}$ pounds. Which is the weight written as an improper fraction?

   A $\frac{1}{64}$ pound   C $\frac{64}{8}$ pounds

   B $\frac{57}{8}$ pounds   D $\frac{65}{8}$ pounds

8. Which mixed number describes the shaded areas?

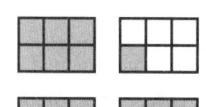

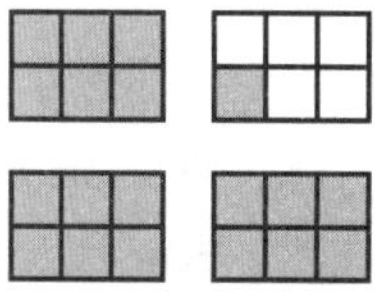

   A $3\frac{1}{6}$ C $3\frac{1}{2}$

   B $3\frac{1}{4}$ D $3\frac{5}{6}$

101

Intervention Practice **H16**

Name _____

Fractions on a Number Line

Circle the correct letter for the answer.

1. Find the fraction for the part of the length that is shaded.

   A $\frac{1}{10}$ **C** $\frac{8}{10}$

   B $\frac{7}{10}$ **D** $\frac{10}{10}$

2. Find the fraction for the part of the length that is shaded.

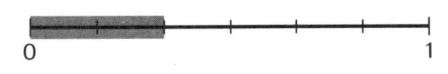

   A $\frac{1}{6}$ **C** $\frac{3}{6}$

   B $\frac{2}{6}$ **D** $\frac{2}{4}$

3. Which letter is at $\frac{3}{7}$ on the number line?

   A R   **C** T

   B S   **D** U

4. Which letter is at $\frac{1}{4}$ on the number line?

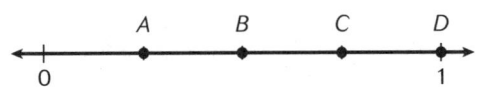

   A A   **C** C

   B B   **D** D

5. Find the fraction for the part of the length that is shaded.

   A $\frac{3}{10}$ **C** $\frac{3}{6}$

   B $\frac{2}{5}$ **D** $\frac{3}{5}$

6. Which letter is at $\frac{4}{9}$ on the number line?

   A J   **C** L

   B K   **D** M

7. Find the fraction for the part of the length that is shaded.

   A $\frac{1}{8}$ **C** $\frac{7}{4}$

   B $\frac{6}{8}$ **D** $1\frac{1}{8}$

8. Which letter is at $\frac{4}{6}$ on the number line?

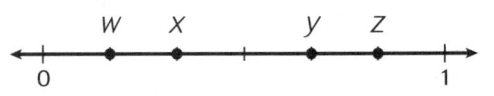

   A W   **C** Y

   B X   **D** Z

Intervention Practice **H17**

Simplest Form

Circle the correct letter for each answer.

1. Which is $\frac{80}{90}$ in simplest form?
   A $\frac{40}{50}$
   B $\frac{7}{8}$
   C $\frac{8}{9}$
   D $\frac{9}{11}$

2. Which is $\frac{15}{25}$ in simplest form?
   A $\frac{2}{5}$
   B $\frac{3}{5}$
   C $\frac{1}{5}$
   D $\frac{2}{7}$

3. Troy made a cake and cut it into 12 equal pieces. Sam ate 3 pieces. In simplest form, what fractional part of the cake did Sam eat?
   A $\frac{3}{12}$
   B $\frac{1}{3}$
   C $\frac{1}{4}$
   D $\frac{2}{3}$

4. Which is $\frac{65}{205}$ in simplest form?
   A $\frac{4}{15}$
   B $\frac{8}{17}$
   C $\frac{12}{39}$
   D $\frac{13}{41}$

5. Which is $\frac{18}{40}$ in simplest form?
   A $\frac{9}{15}$
   B $\frac{9}{20}$
   C $\frac{6}{13}$
   D $\frac{3}{13}$

6. Gina works in a shoe store. During a sale, she sold 42 pairs of shoes. Before the sale started, there were 84 pairs of shoes in stock. In simplest form, what fractional part of the stock did Gina sell?
   A $\frac{1}{4}$
   B $\frac{1}{2}$
   C $\frac{1}{3}$
   D $\frac{1}{6}$

Mr. Ruskins purchased the following new items for his school physical education class.

Item	Number
Jump Rope	4
Baseball	3
Soccer ball	2
Swim fins	1

7. The first grade teacher, borrowed the soccer balls. What fraction of the new equipment did she borrow?
   A $\frac{1}{5}$
   B $\frac{1}{3}$
   C $\frac{1}{4}$
   D $\frac{1}{8}$

Intervention Practice **H18**

Using Number Sense to Compare Fractions

Circle the correct letter for the answer.

1. Compare. $\frac{7}{15}$ ● $\frac{11}{15}$.

   A <   C =
   B >   D +

2. Which fraction is the greatest?

   A $\frac{1}{3}$ C $\frac{5}{8}$
   B $\frac{8}{11}$ D $\frac{4}{7}$

Use the table for Questions 3–4.

Name	Amount of Book Read
Ben	$\frac{4}{9}$
Maria	$\frac{1}{3}$
Samuel	$\frac{5}{6}$
Tuan	$\frac{2}{3}$

3. Assuming everyone is reading the same book, who has read the most?

   A Ben   C Samuel
   B Maria   D Tuan

4. Assuming everyone is reading the same book, who has read the least?

   A Ben   C Samuel
   B Maria   D Tuan

5. A hardware store sells hex nuts in four diameters. Which is the largest?

   A $\frac{5}{16}$ C $\frac{1}{4}$
   B $\frac{1}{8}$ D $\frac{3}{8}$

6. Which fraction is the least?

   A $\frac{2}{7}$ C $\frac{4}{7}$
   B $\frac{4}{5}$ D $\frac{1}{8}$

7. Compare. $\frac{4}{5}$ ● $\frac{3}{4}$.

   A <   C =
   B >   D +

8. If Jim walks $\frac{3}{8}$ mile to school, Li walks $\frac{3}{5}$ mile, and Mark $\frac{3}{7}$ mile, who walks the farthest?

   A Jim   C Mark
   B Li   D all the same

Intervention Practice **H19**

Comparing and Ordering Fractions

Circle the correct letter for the answer.

1. Which list shows the fractions in order from least to greatest?

    A $\frac{4}{4}, \frac{3}{4}, \frac{1}{3}$ C $\frac{3}{4}, \frac{4}{5}, \frac{1}{3}$

    B $\frac{1}{3}, \frac{4}{5}, \frac{3}{4}$ D $\frac{1}{3}, \frac{3}{4}, \frac{4}{5}$

2. Andrew said he ate more than $\frac{1}{2}$ of his sandwich. Which of the following could Andrew not have eaten?

    A $\frac{3}{9}$ C $\frac{5}{8}$

    B $\frac{6}{10}$ D $\frac{2}{3}$

3. Which statement is NOT correct?

    A $\frac{6}{9} = \frac{2}{3}$ C $\frac{3}{4} > \frac{8}{12}$

    B $\frac{5}{6} < \frac{2}{5}$ D $\frac{2}{3} < \frac{13}{15}$

4. Which symbol would complete the statement

    $$4\frac{7}{18} \bullet 4\frac{2}{3}?$$

    A >   C =
    B <   D +

5. Which statement is correct?

    A $3\frac{2}{3} < 3\frac{10}{15}$ C $2\frac{7}{10} < 2\frac{3}{5}$

    B $5\frac{1}{2} < 5\frac{6}{8}$ D $1\frac{3}{5} < 1\frac{6}{20}$

6. Mario correctly identified $\frac{2}{3}$ of the birds that the bird club saw on a walk. Betty identified $\frac{1}{2}$, Tami identified $\frac{3}{5}$, and Saul identified $\frac{11}{15}$. Which person correctly identified the most birds?

    A Mario   C Tami
    B Betty   D Saul

7. The diameters of a set of copper pipes are $\frac{3}{8}$ inch, $\frac{1}{4}$ inch, $\frac{7}{16}$ inch, and $\frac{5}{12}$ inch. Which shows the pipes in order from the least to the greatest diameter?

    A $\frac{5}{12}$ in., $\frac{3}{8}$ in., $\frac{1}{4}$ in., $\frac{7}{16}$ in.

    B $\frac{1}{4}$ in., $\frac{3}{8}$ in., $\frac{5}{12}$ in., $\frac{7}{16}$ in.

    C $\frac{1}{4}$ in., $\frac{3}{8}$ in., $\frac{7}{16}$ in., $\frac{5}{12}$ in.

    D $\frac{5}{12}$ in., $\frac{7}{16}$ in., $\frac{3}{8}$ in., $\frac{1}{4}$ in.

Name _____

Intervention Practice **H20**

Comparing and Ordering Fractions and Mixed Numbers

Circle the correct letter for the answer.

1. Which statement is NOT correct?

   A $2\frac{1}{3} > 2\frac{3}{2}$ **C** $1\frac{5}{7} < 1\frac{7}{5}$

   B $3\frac{4}{5} < 3\frac{6}{5}$ **D** $6\frac{8}{5} > 6\frac{2}{5}$

2. Carlos estimated he spends $2\frac{4}{5}$ hours a day listening to the radio. Which is the mixed number as an improper fraction?

   A $\frac{10}{4}$ **C** $\frac{14}{5}$

   B $2\frac{8}{10}$ **D** $\frac{14}{4}$

3. Choose the correct symbol.

   $\frac{16}{5}$ ● $3\frac{1}{2}$

   A + **C** <
   B > **D** =

4. Chelsea jumped $3\frac{2}{3}$ feet, Mark jumped $3\frac{1}{2}$ feet, Ellen jumped $3\frac{1}{4}$ feet, and Jimmy jumped $3\frac{7}{8}$ feet. Who jumped the farthest?

   A Chelsea
   B Jimmy
   C Mark
   D Ellen

5. What is the mixed number $4\frac{2}{5}$ written as an improper fraction?

   A $\frac{20}{5}$ **C** $\frac{20}{2}$

   B $\frac{22}{5}$ **D** $\frac{22}{2}$

6. Which statement is correct?

   A $\frac{9}{2} > \frac{20}{4}$

   B $\frac{7}{8} > \frac{8}{7}$

   C $\frac{8}{3} < \frac{10}{4}$

   D $\frac{28}{9} < \frac{13}{3}$

7. Which list shows the fractions in order from least to greatest?

   A $1\frac{1}{4}; \frac{32}{6}; \frac{18}{3}; \frac{1}{3}$

   B $\frac{18}{3}; \frac{32}{6}; 1\frac{1}{4}; \frac{1}{3}$

   C $\frac{1}{3}; \frac{18}{3}; \frac{32}{6}; 1\frac{1}{4}$

   D $\frac{1}{3}; 1\frac{1}{4}; \frac{32}{6}; \frac{18}{3}$

8. A carpenter measures a piece of wood. It is $15\frac{1}{4}$ inches long. He wants to write the measurement as an improper fraction. Which fraction should he write?

   A $\frac{16}{4}$ inches **C** $\frac{61}{4}$ inches

   B $\frac{60}{4}$ inches **D** $15\frac{2}{8}$ inches

Intervention Practice **H21**

Fractions and Division

Circle the correct letter for the answer.

1. Mrs. Lopez has 1 apple. She wants her 4 children to share the apple equally. How much will each child get?

   A $\frac{1}{4}$ apple   C $\frac{3}{4}$ apple

   B $\frac{1}{2}$ apple   D 4 apples

2. Find 3 ÷ 10.

   A $\frac{3}{10}$ C $3\frac{1}{10}$

   B $\frac{1}{3}$ D $3\frac{1}{3}$

3. Bagels are sold in packages of 6. Mr. Henderson has 18 bagels. How many packages did Mr. Henderson buy?

   A $\frac{1}{6}$ package   C 2 packages

   B $\frac{6}{18}$ package   D 3 packages

4. Find 7 ÷ 2.

   A $\frac{2}{7}$ C 3

   B $2\frac{1}{2}$ D $3\frac{1}{2}$

5. Find 5 ÷ 7.

   A $1\frac{2}{5}$ C $\frac{7}{5}$

   B $1\frac{2}{7}$ D $\frac{5}{7}$

6. Ryan bought a pound of cheese. He sliced the cheese into 8 equal pieces. How much does each slice weigh?

   A $\frac{1}{10}$ pound   C $\frac{1}{2}$ pound

   B $\frac{1}{8}$ pound   D 1 pound

7. Find 4 ÷ 3.

   A $\frac{3}{4}$ C $1\frac{1}{4}$

   B $1\frac{1}{12}$ D $1\frac{1}{3}$

Name _____

Intervention Practice **H22**

Estimating Fractional Amounts

Circle the correct letter for the answer.

1. 11 of the 20 apples the teacher brought to class were eaten. About what fraction of the apples remains?

    A $\frac{1}{2}$ C $\frac{1}{4}$
    B $\frac{2}{3}$ D $\frac{3}{4}$

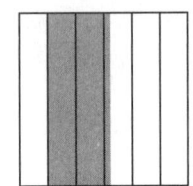

2. Estimate the shaded part.

    A $\frac{3}{4}$ C $\frac{1}{4}$
    B $\frac{1}{3}$ D $\frac{1}{2}$

3. Which figure is about $\frac{2}{3}$ gray?

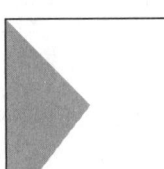

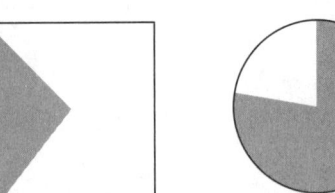

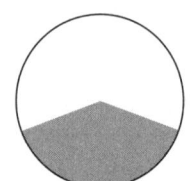

    A   C
    B   D

4. The pet store sold 23 of the 98 parakeets it had. About what fraction of the parakeets remain?

    A $\frac{1}{3}$ C $\frac{3}{4}$
    B $\frac{1}{2}$ D $\frac{1}{4}$

Use the graph for Questions 5 and 6.

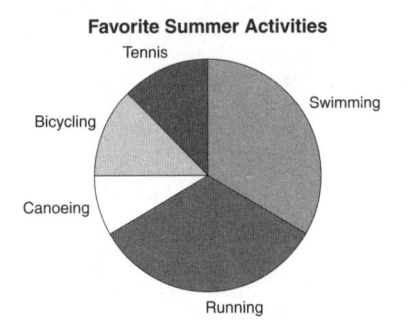

Favorite Summer Activities

5. What fraction of the students surveyed preferred swimming?

    A $\frac{1}{2}$ C $\frac{1}{4}$
    B $\frac{1}{3}$ D $\frac{3}{4}$

6. What fraction of the students surveyed preferred bicycling and tennis combined?

    A $\frac{1}{4}$ C $\frac{3}{4}$
    B $\frac{2}{3}$ D $\frac{1}{2}$

Intervention Practice **H23**

Fractions and Mixed Numbers on the Number Line

Circle the correct letter for the answer.

1. What fraction or mixed number represents point H?

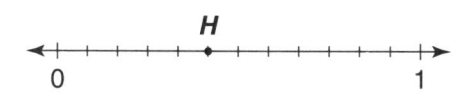

   (number line from 0 to 1 with point H)

   A $\frac{5}{12}$ C $\frac{19}{12}$

   B $\frac{13}{12}$ D $\frac{7}{12}$

2. Which fraction is between $\frac{1}{4}$ and $1\frac{3}{4}$?

   A $\frac{1}{8}$ C $\frac{6}{4}$

   B $\frac{8}{4}$ D $\frac{15}{8}$

3. Order from least to greatest:

   $\frac{3}{13}, \frac{11}{13}, \frac{15}{13}, \frac{7}{13}$

   A $\frac{3}{13}, \frac{15}{13}, \frac{7}{13}, \frac{11}{13}$

   B $\frac{11}{13}, \frac{15}{13}, \frac{7}{13}, \frac{3}{13}$

   C $\frac{7}{13}, \frac{3}{13}, \frac{15}{13}, \frac{11}{13}$

   D $\frac{3}{13}, \frac{7}{13}, \frac{11}{13}, \frac{15}{13}$

4. Which fraction or mixed number represents point J?

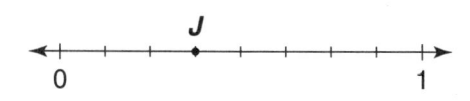

   (number line from 0 to 1 with point J)

   A $\frac{1}{8}$ C $\frac{3}{8}$

   B $1\frac{3}{8}$ D $\frac{7}{8}$

5. While on a camping trip, Tony walked $\frac{5}{8}$ of a mile, Maria walked $\frac{4}{8}$ of a mile, Max walked $\frac{9}{8}$ of a mile, and Lynn walked $\frac{3}{8}$ of a mile. Who walked the greatest distance?

   A Maria   C Tony

   B Lynn   D Max

6. Jordan is planning a trip. He earned $\frac{2}{12}$ of the money he needs by mowing lawns, $\frac{5}{12}$ by raking leaves, $\frac{4}{12}$ by babysitting, and $\frac{1}{12}$ by recycling. Where did he earn most of his money?

   A babysitting
   B mowing lawns
   C raking leaves
   D recycling

7. Which fraction is between $\frac{2}{16}$ and $\frac{21}{16}$?

   A $\frac{1}{16}$ C $\frac{20}{16}$

   B $\frac{26}{16}$ D $\frac{22}{16}$

109

Equivalent Fractions

Circle the correct letter for the answer.

1. Which fraction is equivalent to $\frac{5}{8}$?

   A $\frac{4}{7}$ C $\frac{10}{16}$

   B $\frac{5}{9}$ D $\frac{15}{20}$

2. Which of the following are equivalent fractions for $\frac{6}{18}$?

   A $\frac{1}{3}$ and $\frac{3}{9}$

   B $\frac{1}{3}$ and $\frac{2}{9}$

   C $\frac{1}{4}$ and $\frac{3}{9}$

   D $\frac{1}{4}$ and $\frac{2}{8}$

3. Which number belongs in the ■?

   $2\frac{8}{10} = 2\frac{■}{5}$

   A 3   C 8
   B 4   D 16

4. Which fraction is equivalent to $\frac{2}{3}$?

   A $\frac{2}{6}$ C $\frac{12}{18}$

   B $\frac{2}{4}$ D $\frac{16}{20}$

5. Which fraction is equivalent to $\frac{3}{5}$?

   A $\frac{1}{3}$ C $\frac{6}{10}$

   B $\frac{2}{7}$ D $\frac{9}{12}$

6. At the horse show, 6 of the 10 horses are brown. Which fraction, in simplest form, describes the horses that are brown?

   A $\frac{4}{5}$ C $\frac{1}{2}$

   B $\frac{3}{5}$ D $\frac{3}{10}$

7. Which shows a fraction that names the shaded part of the circle and another fraction that is equivalent to it?

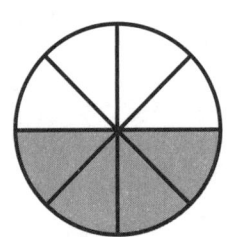

   A $\frac{4}{8}, \frac{1}{2}$ C $\frac{5}{8}, \frac{10}{16}$

   B $\frac{4}{8}, \frac{2}{5}$ D $\frac{4}{8}, \frac{2}{6}$

Intervention Practice **H25**

Relating Fractions and Decimals

Circle the correct letter for the answer.

1. Which fraction and decimal describes the shaded part?

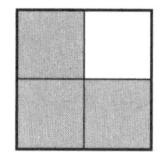

   A $\frac{1}{4}$ and 0.25

   B $\frac{1}{2}$ and 0.5

   C $\frac{3}{4}$ and 0.75

   D $\frac{3}{4}$ and 0.3

2. Which of the following is equal to $\frac{1}{4}$?

   A 0.14   C 0.25
   B 0.20   D 0.40

3. Shawn bought 0.5 pound of strawberries. Which fraction is equal to 0.5?

   A $\frac{1}{50}$ C $\frac{5}{10}$
   B $\frac{1}{5}$ D $\frac{50}{10}$

4. Which of the following is equal to 0.2?

   A $\frac{2}{100}$ C $\frac{1}{2}$
   B $\frac{1}{5}$ D $\frac{2}{1}$

5. Which is a fraction and a decimal for 3 tenths?

   A $\frac{3}{100}$ and 0.03   C $\frac{1}{3}$ and 0.3
   B $\frac{3}{10}$ and 0.3   D $\frac{3}{3}$ and 1

6. Which is a fraction and a decimal for Point P?

   A $\frac{3}{8}$ and 0.375

   B $\frac{4}{8}$ and 0.5

   C $\frac{5}{8}$ and 0.75

   D $\frac{6}{8}$ and 0.75

7. Which is a decimal for 8 hundredths?

   A 0.08   C 8.0
   B 0.8   D 800

8. Which decimal describes the number of faces that are not smiling?

   A 0.2   C 0.6
   B 0.25   D 0.75

111

Fractions, Decimals, and the Number Line

Circle the correct letter for the answer.

1. Find the number shown by each letter.

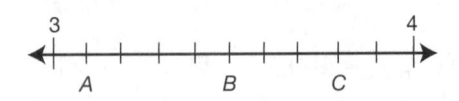

   A A: 3.2, B: 3.5, C: 3.8
   B A: 3.1, B: 3.4, C: 3.8
   C A: 3.1, B: 3.5, C: 3.9
   D A: 3.1, B: 3.5, C: 3.8

2. Which pair of decimals name the same number?

   A 0.5, 0.05
   B 0.7, 0.70
   C 0.77, 0.70
   D 0.08, 0.80

3. Which improper fraction is located at Point M?

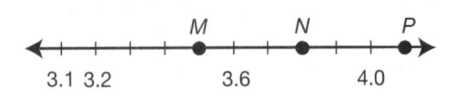

   A $\dfrac{35}{100}$
   B $\dfrac{35}{10}$
   C $\dfrac{37}{10}$
   D $\dfrac{35}{1}$

4. Which letter is located at $\dfrac{63}{100}$?

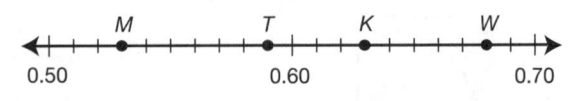

   A K
   B M
   C W
   D Z

5. Which decimal is located at Point A?

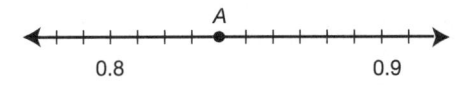

   A 0.804
   B 0.84
   C 8.04
   D 8.4

6. Which mixed number is located at Point S?

   A $5\dfrac{7}{10}$
   B $5\dfrac{9}{10}$
   C $5\dfrac{92}{100}$
   D $6\dfrac{2}{10}$

7. Which decimal is equivalent to $\dfrac{9}{10}$?

   A 0.009
   B 0.09
   C 0.9
   D 9.0

Intervention Practice **H27**

Adding and Subtracting Fractions

Circle the correct letter for the answer.

1. $\dfrac{7}{9}$
   $-\dfrac{4}{9}$

   A $\dfrac{3}{9}$ C $\dfrac{11}{9}$

   B $\dfrac{4}{9}$ D 3

2. $\dfrac{2}{7} + \dfrac{3}{7} =$

   A $\dfrac{5}{14}$ C $\dfrac{5}{7}$

   B $\dfrac{14}{21}$ D $\dfrac{6}{7}$

3. Evan finished $\dfrac{1}{5}$ of his project before he stopped to eat lunch. After lunch, he completed another $\dfrac{1}{5}$ of his project. How much of his project has he completed so far?

   A $\dfrac{1}{10}$ C $\dfrac{1}{5}$

   B $\dfrac{3}{5}$ D $\dfrac{2}{5}$

4. Beth ate $\dfrac{3}{8}$ of the plums on Monday and $\dfrac{2}{8}$ of the plums on Tuesday. How many of the plums did Beth eat?

   A $\dfrac{1}{16}$ of the plums

   B $\dfrac{1}{8}$ of the plums

   C $\dfrac{5}{16}$ of the plums

   D $\dfrac{5}{8}$ of the plums

5. Mario used $\dfrac{7}{10}$ yard of rope for his project. Sam used $\dfrac{5}{10}$ yard of rope for his project. How much more rope did Mario use?

   A $\dfrac{2}{10}$ yard   C $\dfrac{12}{10}$ yard

   B $\dfrac{5}{10}$ yard   D 2 yards

6. $\dfrac{3}{8} + \dfrac{4}{8} =$

   A $\dfrac{5}{8}$ C $\dfrac{7}{16}$

   B $\dfrac{7}{8}$ D $\dfrac{7}{24}$

Intervention Practice **H28**

Estimating Fraction Sums and Differences

Circle the correct letter for the answer.

1. $\frac{3}{4} - \frac{3}{8} \bigcirc \frac{1}{2}$

   A <
   B +
   C −
   D >

2. Carol ran $\frac{1}{2}$ mile in the morning and $\frac{1}{4}$ mile in the afternoon. Which statement is true?

   A Carol ran more than 1 mile in all.
   B Carol ran less than 1 mile in all.
   C Carol ran exactly 1 mile in all.
   D Carol ran less than $\frac{1}{2}$ mile in all.

3. $\frac{1}{6} + \frac{2}{3} \bigcirc 1$

   A <
   B +
   C −
   D >

4. Which statement is true?

   A The sum of $\frac{1}{12}$ and $\frac{5}{12}$ is greater than 1.
   B The sum of $\frac{1}{12}$ and $\frac{5}{12}$ is less than 1.
   C The sum of $\frac{1}{12}$ and $\frac{5}{12}$ is equal to 1.
   D The sum of $\frac{1}{12}$ and $\frac{5}{12}$ is greater than 2.

5. $\frac{2}{3} - \frac{1}{4} \bigcirc \frac{1}{2}$

   A <
   B +
   C −
   D >

6. $\frac{7}{12} + \frac{7}{12} \bigcirc 1$

   A <
   B +
   C −
   D >

7. Estimate one half-hour minus one quarter-hour.

   A More than one half-hour
   B Less than one half-hour
   C More than one hour
   D Less than one quarter hour

8. $\frac{3}{4} \bigcirc \frac{3}{4} > 1$

   A <
   B −
   C +
   D >

9. Juan ate $\frac{1}{2}$ of a pizza. Sara ate $\frac{3}{8}$ of a pizza. Which estimate shows the amount of pizza they ate?

   A $\frac{1}{2} + \frac{3}{8} > 1$
   B $\frac{1}{2} - \frac{3}{8} < \frac{1}{2}$
   C $\frac{1}{2} + \frac{3}{8} < 1$
   D $\frac{1}{2} + \frac{3}{8} < \frac{1}{2}$

Name _____

Intervention Practice **H29**

Math Diagnosis and Intervention System

Adding and Subtracting Fractions with Like Denominators

Circle the correct letter for the answer.

1. $\frac{7}{9}$
   $-\frac{4}{9}$

   A $\frac{3}{9}$ C $\frac{11}{9}$

   B $\frac{4}{9}$ D 3

2. $\frac{2}{7} + \frac{3}{7} =$

   A $\frac{5}{14}$ C $\frac{5}{7}$

   B $\frac{14}{21}$ D $\frac{6}{7}$

3. Evan finished $\frac{1}{5}$ of his project before he stopped to eat lunch. After lunch, he completed another $\frac{1}{5}$ of his project. How much of his project has he completed so far?

   A $\frac{1}{10}$ C $\frac{1}{5}$

   B $\frac{3}{5}$ D $\frac{2}{5}$

4. Beth ate $\frac{3}{8}$ of the plums on Monday and $\frac{2}{8}$ of the plums on Tuesday. How many of the plums did Beth eat?

   A $\frac{1}{16}$ of the plums

   B $\frac{1}{8}$ of the plums

   C $\frac{5}{16}$ of the plums

   D $\frac{5}{8}$ of the plums

5. Mario used $\frac{7}{10}$ yard of rope for his project. Sam used $\frac{5}{10}$ yard of rope for his project. How much more rope did Mario use?

   A $\frac{2}{10}$ yard   C $\frac{12}{10}$ yard

   B $\frac{5}{10}$ yard   D 2 yards

6. $\frac{3}{8} + \frac{4}{8} =$

   A $\frac{5}{8}$ C $\frac{7}{16}$

   B $\frac{7}{12}$ D $\frac{7}{8}$

115

Least Common Denominator

Circle the correct letter for the answer.

1. Find the LCD of $\frac{1}{12}$ and $\frac{7}{30}$.
   - A 6
   - B 24
   - C 30
   - D 60

2. In gym class, Adrian ran $\frac{7}{8}$ of a mile and Juana ran $\frac{5}{12}$ of a mile. What is the least common denominator of the fractions?
   - A 6
   - B 12
   - C 24
   - D 36

3. At dinner, Nik and Katie ate $\frac{1}{2}$ of a roast. Later Nik ate another $\frac{1}{6}$ of the roast. What is the least common denominator of the fractions?
   - A 2
   - B 6
   - C 8
   - D 12

4. Find the LCD of $\frac{1}{21}$ and $\frac{3}{28}$.
   - A 7
   - B 48
   - C 84
   - D 588

5. Find the LCD of $\frac{3}{4}$ and $\frac{2}{10}$.
   - A 2
   - B 10
   - C 20
   - D 40

6. Jefferson Contracting painted $\frac{1}{3}$ of a building on Monday. On Tuesday they completed another $\frac{1}{5}$ of the building. What is the least common denominator of the fractions?
   - A 10
   - B 15
   - C 20
   - D 30

7. Find the LCD for $\frac{3}{9}$ and $\frac{4}{15}$.
   - A 3
   - B 36
   - C 45
   - D 60

8. Members of the Parents' Club divided the work for various jobs at the school carnival. So far, Mr. Alvarez has completed $\frac{7}{8}$ of his job. Ms. Diem has completed $\frac{5}{12}$ of her work. Mr. Hannula has completed $\frac{1}{4}$ of his work. What is the least common denominator for the three fractions?
   - A 4
   - B 8
   - C 12
   - D 24

Intervention Practice **H31**

Adding and Subtracting Fractions with Unlike Denominators

Circle the correct letter for the answer.

1. $\dfrac{5}{6} - \dfrac{2}{3} =$

   A $\dfrac{3}{3}$ C $\dfrac{1}{6}$

   B $\dfrac{3}{6}$ D $\dfrac{2}{18}$

2. On Monday, Lacy ran $\dfrac{2}{5}$ mile. On Tuesday, she ran $\dfrac{3}{10}$ mile. How far did she run all together?

   A $\dfrac{5}{5}$ C $\dfrac{5}{10}$

   B $\dfrac{7}{10}$ D $\dfrac{4}{10}$

3. Jason ate $\dfrac{1}{4}$ of the fruit salad. Tony ate $\dfrac{3}{8}$ of the fruit salad. How much more did Tony eat than Jason?

   A $\dfrac{1}{8}$ more C $\dfrac{4}{8}$ more

   B $\dfrac{2}{8}$ more D $\dfrac{5}{8}$ more

4. $\dfrac{5}{12} + \dfrac{1}{3} =$

   A $\dfrac{6}{12}$ C $\dfrac{8}{12}$

   B $\dfrac{7}{12}$ D $\dfrac{9}{12}$

5. Which operation would you use to solve this problem?

   Mark ran $\dfrac{3}{4}$ mile. Lupe ran $\dfrac{4}{5}$ mile. How much farther did Lupe run than Mark?

   A Addition
   B Subtraction
   C Multiplication
   D Division

6. $\dfrac{1}{2} + \dfrac{1}{8} =$

   A $\dfrac{2}{8}$ C $\dfrac{5}{8}$

   B $\dfrac{2}{4}$ D $\dfrac{2}{2}$

Math Diagnosis and Intervention System

Name _____

Intervention Practice **H32**

Investigating Adding and Subtracting Mixed Numbers

Circle the correct letter for the answer.

1. Kendra bought $7\frac{1}{8}$ pounds of apples and $3\frac{3}{8}$ pounds of bananas. How many more pounds of apples did she buy?

   A $4\frac{1}{4}$ pounds
   B $10\frac{1}{2}$ pounds
   C $4\frac{1}{2}$ pounds
   D $3\frac{3}{4}$ pounds

2. $8\frac{5}{6} + 3\frac{5}{6} =$

   A $12\frac{2}{3}$ C $11\frac{5}{6}$
   B $12\frac{1}{3}$ D $11\frac{1}{2}$

3. $9\frac{2}{5} - 3\frac{4}{5} =$

   A $5\frac{4}{5}$ C $5\frac{3}{5}$
   B $6\frac{2}{5}$ D $6\frac{1}{2}$

4. Jean bought $5\frac{1}{4}$ pounds of hamburger and $3\frac{3}{4}$ pounds of sausage. How many pounds of meat did she buy?

   A $2\frac{1}{2}$ pounds
   B $8\frac{1}{2}$ pounds
   C 9 pounds
   D $9\frac{1}{4}$ pounds

5. Mary bought $3\frac{1}{8}$ yards of blue ribbon. She uses $2\frac{7}{8}$ yards of ribbon. How many yards of ribbon does she have left?

   A 5 yards   C $\frac{1}{2}$ yard
   B 6 yards   D $\frac{1}{4}$ yard

Use the table for Questions 6–7.

Animal	Height of Animal
Nyala	$45\frac{4}{16}$ inches
Lion	$47\frac{4}{16}$ inches
Blue Wildebeest	$59\frac{1}{16}$ inches
Buffalo	$55\frac{2}{16}$ inches
Eland	$66\frac{15}{16}$ inches

Source: *Columbia Encyclopedia, 6th ed.*

6. What is the difference in height between a blue wildebeest and an eland?

   A $7\frac{7}{8}$ in.   C $8\frac{1}{16}$ in.
   B $7\frac{13}{16}$ in.   D $8\frac{1}{2}$ in.

7. What is the combined height of a nyala and a lion?

   A $92\frac{1}{2}$ in.   C $91\frac{1}{16}$ in.
   B 92 in.   D 2 in.

118

Intervention Practice **H33**

Estimating Sums and Differences of Mixed Numbers

Circle the correct letter for the answer.

1. Dave is combining $1\frac{3}{4}$ quarts of soda and $1\frac{7}{8}$ quarts of juice to make punch. About what size container will he need to mix the punch?

   A About 1 quart
   B About 2 quarts
   C About 3 quarts
   D About 4 quarts

2. Which is the best estimate for $9\frac{1}{5} - 4\frac{7}{8}$?

   A About 14   C About 5
   B About 13   D About 4

3. Which is the best estimate for $2\frac{5}{6} + 2\frac{1}{8}$?

   A About 4   C About 6
   B About 5   D About 7

4. Hanna has $4\frac{4}{5}$ pounds of apples. Megan has $2\frac{9}{10}$ pounds of apples. About how many pounds of apples do the girls have together?

   A About 5 pounds
   B About 6 pounds
   C About 8 pounds
   D About 9 pounds

5. Which is the best estimate for $7\frac{1}{3} - 4\frac{1}{4}$?

   A About 2   C About 4
   B About 3   D About 5

6. Jamie's cat weighs $6\frac{1}{4}$ pounds. Her dog weighs $9\frac{7}{8}$ pounds. About how much more does Jamie's dog weigh than her cat?

   A About 3 pounds
   B About 4 pounds
   C About 5 pounds
   D About 6 pounds

7. Which is the best estimate for $5 + 1\frac{5}{8}$?

   A About 5   C About 7
   B About 6   D About 8

8. Greg planted $2\frac{1}{4}$ acres of wheat. Erin planted $3\frac{1}{3}$ acres of wheat. About how many acres of wheat did they plant in all?

   A About 5 acres
   B About 6 acres
   C About 7 acres
   D About 8 acres

119

Intervention Practice **H34**

Adding Mixed Numbers

Circle the correct letter for the answer.

1. Kira gave handball lessons for $5\frac{3}{4}$ hours on Saturday and $3\frac{2}{3}$ hours on Sunday. How many hours did she work in all?

   A $10\frac{5}{12}$ hours   C $8\frac{5}{12}$ hours

   B $9\frac{5}{12}$ hours   D $2\frac{1}{12}$ hours

2. $3\frac{1}{4} + 2\frac{5}{6} =$

   A $5\frac{1}{12}$ C 6

   B $5\frac{23}{24}$ D $6\frac{1}{12}$

3. Sally has $6\frac{5}{8}$ cups of orange juice in one container and $4\frac{2}{3}$ cups in another. How much orange juice does she have in all?

   A $10\frac{7}{24}$ cups

   B $11\frac{1}{4}$ cups

   C $11\frac{7}{24}$ cups

   D $11\frac{1}{3}$ cups

4. $4\frac{1}{4} + 7\frac{4}{5} =$

   A $5\frac{6}{11}$ C $6\frac{1}{18}$

   B $5\frac{17}{18}$ D $12\frac{1}{20}$

5. Gina needs $3\frac{5}{6}$ cups of milk for one recipe and $1\frac{1}{8}$ cups of milk for another. How much milk does she need in all?

   A $4\frac{3}{4}$ cups   C $4\frac{11}{12}$ cups

   B $4\frac{5}{6}$ cups   D $4\frac{23}{24}$ cups

6. $2\frac{1}{3} + 4\frac{3}{4} =$

   A $7\frac{1}{3}$ C $6\frac{1}{12}$

   B $7\frac{1}{12}$ D $6\frac{4}{12}$

7. $3\frac{2}{5}$
   $+ 4\frac{1}{3}$

   A $8\frac{11}{15}$ C $7\frac{3}{5}$

   B $7\frac{11}{15}$ D $7\frac{3}{8}$

Intervention Practice **H35**

Subtracting Mixed Numbers

Circle the correct letter for the answer.

1. $4\frac{7}{8} - 2\frac{3}{4} =$

   A $1\frac{1}{8}$ C $2\frac{1}{8}$

   B $1\frac{1}{2}$ D $2\frac{1}{2}$

2. At the fruit stand, fruit is sold by the pound. Chan bought $4\frac{1}{6}$ pounds of apples. Shannon bought $1\frac{3}{4}$ pounds of strawberries and $2\frac{1}{4}$ pounds of apples. How many more pounds of apples did Chan buy than Shannon?

   A $\frac{11}{12}$ pound   C $1\frac{5}{6}$ pounds

   B $1\frac{2}{3}$ pounds   D $1\frac{11}{12}$ pounds

3. $6\frac{1}{3} - 5\frac{4}{5} =$

   A $\frac{8}{15}$ C $1\frac{8}{15}$

   B $\frac{11}{15}$ D $12\frac{1}{15}$

4. Mason had 10 yards of material. He used $3\frac{7}{8}$ yards on a kite. How much material does Mason have left?

   A $6\frac{1}{10}$ yards   C $6\frac{1}{2}$ yards

   B $6\frac{1}{8}$ yards   D $7\frac{1}{8}$ yards

5. Mrs. Quinn must work 8 hours. She has already worked $3\frac{3}{4}$ hours today. How many more hours must she work?

   A $4\frac{1}{4}$ hours   C $5\frac{1}{4}$ hours

   B $4\frac{3}{4}$ hours   D $5\frac{3}{4}$ hours

6. Jan is $4\frac{7}{8}$ feet tall. Her younger sister is $3\frac{1}{2}$ feet tall. How much taller is Jan than her younger sister?

   A $2\frac{5}{8}$ feet   C $1\frac{5}{8}$ feet

   B $2\frac{1}{8}$ feet   D $1\frac{3}{8}$ feet

Math Diagnosis and Intervention System

Intervention Practice **H36**

Name _____

Choose a Computation Method

Circle the correct letter for the answer.

1. Use paper and pencil to find $4\frac{3}{8} + 7\frac{5}{24}$.

   A $11\frac{8}{32}$ C $11\frac{7}{12}$

   B $11\frac{8}{24}$ D $2\frac{5}{6}$

Use the dessert recipe for Questions 2–3.

Fruit	Amount
Strawberries	$4\frac{1}{2}$ pints
Blueberries	$2\frac{1}{4}$ pints
Raspberries	$1\frac{2}{3}$ pint

2. How many more pints of strawberries are needed than raspberries?

   A $2\frac{5}{6}$ C $2\frac{1}{4}$

   B $\frac{7}{12}$ D $6\frac{1}{6}$

3. Which is the total amount, in pints, of berries needed for the recipe?

   A $6\frac{3}{4}$ C $3\frac{11}{12}$

   B $8\frac{5}{12}$ D $1\frac{2}{3}$

4. Use mental math to find $11\frac{5}{7} - 8\frac{3}{7}$.

   A $20\frac{1}{7}$ C $4\frac{2}{7}$

   B $19\frac{2}{7}$ D $3\frac{2}{7}$

5. You have a piece of fabric $6\frac{3}{4}$ yards long. The project you are using it for requires $6\frac{5}{8}$ yards. Use mental math to determine how much fabric you will have left.

   A $13\frac{3}{8}$ yd   C $\frac{1}{8}$ yd

   B $\frac{1}{2}$ yd   D $\frac{1}{4}$ yd

6. A submarine is at a depth of $762\frac{2}{3}$ feet below sea level. Seven minutes later, it is at a depth of $486\frac{1}{8}$ feet below sea level. What is the change in the depth in feet of the submarine?

   A $1{,}248\frac{3}{11}$ C $1{,}248\frac{19}{24}$

   B $276\frac{1}{5}$ D $276\frac{13}{24}$

7. Find $7\frac{1}{3} + 6\frac{5}{6} + 8\frac{3}{4}$.

   A $15\frac{7}{12}$ C $22\frac{11}{22}$

   B $16\frac{1}{2}$ D $21\frac{9}{16}$

122

Name _____

Intervention Practice **H37**

Math Diagnosis and Intervention System

Multiplying Fractions by Whole Numbers

Circle the correct letter for the answer.

---

1. An extra large pizza from Pizzaland is cut into 16 pieces. If Rebecca eats $\frac{1}{4}$ of the pizza, how many pieces has she eaten?

   A 2   **C** 4
   B 3   **D** 48

---

2. A three-pound jar of mixed nuts states that $\frac{1}{8}$ of the nuts are peanuts. How many ounces are peanuts? (Hint: 16 ounces = 1 pound)

   A 8 oz   **C** 4 oz
   B 6 oz   **D** 3 oz

---

3. An adult dosage of cough medicine is 2 tablespoons. The dosage for a six-year-old is $\frac{2}{3}$ that of an adult. How many teaspoons is the dosage for a six-year-old child? (Hint: 3 teaspoons = 1 tablespoon)

   A $1\frac{1}{3}$ **C** 4
   B $2\frac{2}{3}$ **D** 12

---

4. What is $\frac{7}{8}$ of 56?

   A 392   **C** 54
   B 56   **D** 49

---

5. A recipe calls for $\frac{3}{4}$ cup of cocoa to make a batch of cookies. You want to make $\frac{1}{6}$ of a batch. How many tablespoons of cocoa should you use? (Hint: $\frac{1}{4}$ cup = 4 tablespoons)

   A 2   **C** 4
   B 3   **D** 6

---

6. What is $\frac{5}{9}$ of 108?

   A 12   **C** 60
   B 21   **D** 194

---

7. A son is $\frac{2}{5}$ the age of his mother. The mother is 55 years old. How old is the son?

   A 11   **C** 25
   B 22   **D** 33

---

8. A book contains 128 pages. If you have read $\frac{3}{4}$ of the book, how many pages have you read?

   A 32   **C** 96
   B 42   **D** 114

Name _____

Intervention Practice **H38**

Estimating Products

Circle the correct letter for the answer.

1. Estimate $3\frac{7}{8} \times 2\frac{11}{12}$.

   A About 6   C About 9
   B About 8   D About 12

2. Use estimation to find which product has the greatest value.

   A $\frac{3}{4} \times 240$ C $\frac{7}{8} \times 160$
   B $\frac{1}{2} \times 200$ D $\frac{2}{5} \times 100$

3. The teacher will use a decorative border around a square bulletin board. Each side of the bulletin board is $3\frac{7}{8}$ feet long. About how long will the decorative border have to be?

   A About 12 ft   C About 16 ft
   B About 13 ft   D About 20 ft

4. There are 663 students in Oak Hill School. If $\frac{1}{3}$ of the students ride the school bus, about how many students ride the school bus?

   A About 110 students
   B About 220 students
   C About 230 students
   D About 280 students

5. The food committee is deciding how many of each sandwich to make for the school picnic. $\frac{1}{8}$ of the students in the school said they wanted a peanut butter sandwich. There are 478 students in the school. About how many peanut butter sandwiches should the committee make?

   A About 50 peanut butter sandwiches
   B About 60 peanut butter sandwiches
   C About 70 peanut butter sandwiches
   D About 80 peanut butter sandwiches

6. Estimate $12\frac{3}{4} \times 2\frac{1}{12}$.

   A About 12   C About 26
   B About 20   D About 36

7. In getting ready for a 2 mile run, Sara ran $10\frac{1}{5}$ miles a week. To get ready for a 10-kilometer run, she ran $2\frac{3}{4}$ times as far each week. About how far did she run each week to get ready for the 10-kilometer run?

   A About 10 miles
   B About 20 miles
   C About 25 miles
   D About 30 miles

Intervention Practice **H39**

Multiplying by a Fraction

Circle the correct letter for the answer.

1. $\frac{2}{5} \times \frac{4}{9} =$

   A $\frac{1}{2}$ C $\frac{8}{45}$

   B $\frac{3}{7}$ D $\frac{2}{15}$

2. There are 32 apples in a basket. One fourth of them are green. How many apples are green?

   A 8 apples   C 4 apples

   B 6 apples   D 2 apples

3. There are 36 inches in a yard. How many inches are in $\frac{1}{4}$ of a yard?

   A 4 inches   C 9 inches

   B 8 inches   D 18 inches

4. Find the product of $\frac{4}{7}$ and $\frac{7}{8}$.

   A $\frac{3}{5}$ C $\frac{24}{56}$

   B $\frac{3}{56}$ D $\frac{1}{2}$

5. One pizza had onions on $\frac{1}{2}$ of the slices. During the party, $\frac{2}{3}$ of these slices were eaten. What fraction of the whole pizza was this?

   A $\frac{1}{6}$ C $\frac{9}{16}$

   B $\frac{1}{3}$ D $\frac{9}{10}$

6. Which has the greatest value?

   A $\frac{2}{3}$ of 24   C $\frac{3}{4}$ of 12

   B $\frac{3}{8}$ of 48   D $\frac{5}{6}$ of 12

7. $\frac{1}{3} \times \frac{1}{4} =$

   A $\frac{1}{12}$ C $\frac{2}{7}$

   B $\frac{1}{6}$ D $\frac{3}{4}$

8. Find $\frac{5}{8}$ of 14.

   A $7\frac{3}{4}$ C $8\frac{1}{2}$

   B 8   D $8\frac{3}{4}$

Multiplying Fractions and Mixed Numbers

Circle the correct letter for the answer.

1. $\frac{7}{8} \times 5\frac{1}{3} =$

   A $4\frac{2}{3}$ C 10

   B $7\frac{5}{24}$ D $36\frac{1}{8}$

2. Find the product of $4\frac{1}{4}$ and $3\frac{1}{3}$.

   A $12\frac{5}{6}$ C $14\frac{1}{2}$

   B $14\frac{1}{6}$ D $\frac{170}{7}$

3. $\frac{3}{4} \times \frac{11}{18} =$

   A $\frac{1}{3}$ C $\frac{7}{11}$

   B $\frac{11}{24}$ D $\frac{11}{16}$

4. Whitney ordered $4\frac{1}{2}$ dozen rolls for the family reunion. She ordered $1\frac{1}{2}$ as many pats of butter. How many dozen pats of butter did she order?

   A $5\frac{3}{4}$ dozen   C $6\frac{3}{4}$ dozen

   B 6 dozen   D 7 dozen

5. Mr. Henry bought $9\frac{1}{2}$ pounds of bird seed at the garden shop. Mrs. Engle bought $2\frac{1}{2}$ times as much bird seed. How many pounds of bird seed did Mrs. Engle buy?

   A $23\frac{3}{4}$ pounds   C $22\frac{3}{4}$ pounds

   B $23\frac{1}{4}$ pounds   D 18 pounds

6. At Knox Middle School, 120 students play soccer. Of the soccer players, $\frac{2}{3}$ are girls. How many girls play soccer?

   A 40 girls   C 80 girls

   B 60 girls   D 100 girls

7. $\frac{16}{35} \times \frac{7}{40} =$

   A $\frac{1}{3}$ C $\frac{4}{15}$

   B $\frac{1}{4}$ D $\frac{2}{25}$

8. $15 + \left(2\frac{1}{3} \times \frac{11}{4}\right) =$

   A $21\frac{5}{12}$ C 17

   B $17\frac{1}{12}$ D $12\frac{1}{12}$

Name _____

Intervention Practice **H41**

Understanding Division with Fractions

Circle the correct letter for the answer.

1. You cut a pie into 8 pieces. Then you decide to cut each piece in half. How many pieces will you have?

   A 3   **C** 2
   B 4   **D** 16

2. A bread recipe calls for 5 cups of flour. If you add flour to the dough $\frac{1}{4}$ cup at a time, how many times will you add flour to the dough?

   A $\frac{5}{4}$ **C** 10
   B 20   **D** 15

3. How many $\frac{1}{8}$s are in 2?

   A $\frac{1}{16}$ **C** 8
   B $\frac{2}{8}$ **D** 16

4. How many $\frac{1}{4}$s are in 4?

   A $\frac{1}{4}$ **C** $\frac{2}{4}$
   B 16   **D** 44

5. What is $4 \div \frac{4}{9}$?

   A 8   **C** 36
   B 16   **D** 9

6. How many $\frac{3}{4}$-inch nails lying end to end equal 6 inches?

   A 6   **C** 24
   B 8   **D** 26

7. What is $6 \div \frac{2}{3}$?

   A 4   **C** 9
   B 12   **D** 18

8. Kendra has 16 pints of blueberries. If she wants to divide them into half pints, how many will she have?

   A 4   **C** 32
   B 8   **D** 22

Dividing Fractions

Circle the correct letter for the answer.

1. Patrice made 3 cups of pudding. She is serving the pudding in pastry tarts that hold $\frac{1}{4}$ cup each. How many tarts can she fill?

   A $\frac{3}{4}$ tart   C 9 tarts
   B 7 tarts   D 12 tarts

2. $\frac{3}{4} \div \frac{1}{12} =$

   A 12   C 4
   B 9   D 3

3. How many $\frac{3}{4}$-inch patches are needed to make a 36-inch row?

   A 48 patches   C 42 patches
   B 46 patches   D 40 patches

4. $\frac{5}{8} \div \frac{2}{3} =$

   A $\frac{5}{12}$ C $\frac{15}{16}$
   B $\frac{7}{8}$ D $1\frac{1}{16}$

5. Mr. Robinson has $\frac{9}{10}$ pound of clay. He needs to divide it between 3 students. What fraction of a pound of clay will each student get?

   A $\frac{2}{10}$ pound   C $\frac{4}{10}$ pound
   B $\frac{3}{10}$ pound   D $\frac{1}{2}$ pound

6. $5 \div \frac{5}{7} =$

   A 35   C $3\frac{4}{7}$
   B 7   D $\frac{1}{7}$

7. $\frac{7}{10} \div \frac{2}{5} =$

   A $\frac{7}{25}$ C $1\frac{1}{4}$
   B $\frac{4}{7}$ D $1\frac{3}{4}$

8. A cookie recipe calls for $\frac{3}{4}$ cup of sugar. Paco is making the recipe for half the amount. How much sugar does he need?

   A $\frac{3}{8}$ cup   C $\frac{2}{3}$ cup
   B $\frac{1}{2}$ cup   D $1\frac{1}{2}$ cups

Intervention Practice **H43**

Multiplying and Dividing Mixed Numbers

Circle the correct letter for the answer.

1. Eric used $2\frac{1}{2}$ pounds of apples for a pie. He used $1\frac{1}{4}$ times as much fruit in a cobbler. How much fruit did he use in the cobbler?

   A $5\frac{5}{8}$ pounds   C $3\frac{3}{4}$ pounds

   B $4\frac{1}{8}$ pounds   D $3\frac{1}{8}$ pounds

2. $8 \div 3\frac{5}{6} =$

   A $30\frac{2}{3}$ C $2\frac{2}{23}$

   B 20   D $1\frac{2}{3}$

3. $4\frac{1}{2} \times 2\frac{4}{5} =$

   A $7\frac{3}{10}$ C $12\frac{3}{5}$

   B $8\frac{2}{5}$ D $13\frac{3}{5}$

4. Marlene served 8 people $1\frac{2}{3}$ cups of rice pudding each. How much rice pudding did she serve in all?

   A $13\frac{1}{3}$ cups   C $11\frac{1}{3}$ cups

   B $12\frac{2}{3}$ cups   D $8\frac{2}{3}$ cups

5. Maria has $8\frac{3}{4}$ yards of material. Each pillow needs $1\frac{1}{4}$ yards. How many pillows will Maria be able to make?

   A 3 pillows   C 6 pillows

   B 5 pillows   D 7 pillows

6. $\frac{2}{5} \times 1\frac{2}{3} =$

   A $\frac{2}{4}$ C $\frac{2}{3}$

   B $\frac{3}{5}$ D $\frac{7}{15}$

7. Edgar has $3\frac{3}{4}$ pounds of pecans. He is going to put them in 3 separate bags. How many pounds will he put in each bag?

   A $\frac{1}{4}$ pound   C $1\frac{1}{5}$ pounds

   B $\frac{3}{4}$ pound   D $1\frac{1}{4}$ pounds

8. $3\frac{1}{8} \div 1\frac{1}{4} =$

   A $1\frac{9}{22}$ C $3\frac{29}{32}$

   B $2\frac{1}{2}$ D 10